The Television Scripts of Philip Rapp

by Philip Rapp

edited by Ben Ohmart

THE TELEVISION SCRIPTS OF PHILIP RAPP

© 2007 Paul Rapp

All rights reserved.
No part of this book may be reproduced in any form or by any means, electronic, mechanical, digital, photocopying or recording, except for the inclusion in a review, without permission in writing from the the publisher.

Published in the USA by Bear Manor Media
PO Box 71426
Albany, GA 31708

www.Bearmanormedia.com
1-800-566-1251 (Order line only)

ISBN10: 1-59393-070-4
ISBN13: 978-1-59393-070-7

Printed in the United States

Book Design and Typesetting by Jill Ronsley, suneditwrite.com
Cover Design by Paula Tarver-Leckey & Jill Ronsley

CONTENTS

Editor's Note 1

Deputy Seraph 3
   Starring the Marx Brothers

Joan of Arkansas 61
   Starring Joan Davis

Squeegee 115
   Starring Ben Blue

EDITOR'S NOTE

PHILIP RAPP will always be immortal through his catty creation, The Bickersons, an insanely funny radio vignette that also emerged on TV, stage and has influenced a generation of *Honeymooners*-loving viewers. But he was a *far* more prolific author than that. In researching the life of Philip Rapp for his upcoming biography, I was allowed to peruse this very clever man's entire output of scripts, unearthing enough material to write an entire history on The Bickersons and two books of Bickersons scripts that have already seen the light of print. There were also enough yuks to birth the first of ten Baby Snooks script books, and a joke book from his vast joke file!

Though many radio fans know of his writing for Snooks and Bix, little has been written of Rapp's venture into television. Like many writers/directors then and now, he wrote a *lot*, and wrote a lot on spec, sometimes clicking, sometimes not with the Powers That Bought. He directed Wally Cox's short-lived adventure/comedy *The Adventures of Hiram Holiday*, until it was finally one of many shows axed in competition with Disney's stalwart *Wonderful World of Disney*. But *HH* would be one of Rapp's few pilots that would fly further than a filmed first show. This book is intended to be a collection of some of the more interesting and name-worthy pilots that also failed to fly, but deserve to be read.

I talk more about these series in my Phil Rapp biography, but briefly:

In late 1958 Rapp pitched an idea for a series called *Deputy Seraph*, starring the Marx Brothers, which would wind up being their penultimate appearance on film together. Harpo and Chico were immediately on board to play angels involved in each week's story, with Groucho signing a heavenly contract later. Only a few minutes of their scene was shot, however, as were the photos inside this book, and nothing else. The project was scrapped too quickly once Chico failed to pass the medical physical required for insuring its stars during the series. Those few minutes have wound up on

DVD since then, but this is the first public viewing of their entire divine adventure.

Around the same time, Joan filmed her adventure-comedy pilot of *Joan of Arkansas*, about a dental assistant who is press-ganged into government service, but the series failed to sell, and also ended up being the last appearance of that star on film.

Squeegee was a pilot written for comedian Ben Blue around 1954, and filmed in April of 1955, around the same time that Rapp was trying to sell the residual rights to the 78 *Topper* episodes he owned (having directed or produced a number of them). It was his *Topper* hit that helped Rapp get the funding he needed for several of these later pilots that failed to catch on.

Rapp was a deeply funny and prolific writer who deserves to be remembered as more than the creator of the Bickersons. This should do it!

Ben Ohmart
September 2006

DEPUTY SERAPH

Starring the Marx Brothers

PROLOGUE

FADE IN:

LONG SHOT — EXT. STAR-STUDDED SKY — NIGHT

Heavenly music is HEARD as the CAMERA ZOOMS rapidly up a beam of light apparently originating in the Milky Way. Up we travel until a tiny figure is discernible among the ever larger-growing constellations. Now we make it out to be a white-robed angel reverently fingering a golden harp. The head is completely obscured by the frame of the instrument, and the CAMERA, eager to discover the identity of the heavenly harpist, CIRCLES the player, MOVES IN and comes to rest on.

HEAD SHOT — HARPO MARX

His face rendered seraphic from his art, but the rest of him as ludicrous as ever. The battered high hat, resting precariously on the improbable blond curls, the walking stick topped with the old auto horn, the disreputable shoes — only the accepted white robe to confirm the fact that you're looking at an angel on his home cloud. Almost imperceptibly a piano has joined Harpo in accompaniment and the

ANGLE WIDENS

To include CHICO... He is seated at a small spinet supported by nothing. Chico, his elfin face clothed in a beatific smile, accompanies Harpo, his fingers caressing the keys as the duo continue with the *saintly theme*. Chico, too, is in the celestial uniform, but also wears his pointy little hat, jauntily balanced on his black curls.

MED SHOT — CHICO AND HARPO

As they play. Without warning, and taking the listener completely by surprise, they have modulated into a *jivey number*. OVER THIS the TITLES appear. As each name appears on the screen we CUT to a single of the player.

CHICO MARX
as
ANGEL 2nd CLASS

HARPO MARX
as
ABLE-BODIED CHERUB

A SIREN is HEARD above the music and we

DISSOLVE:

MED SHOT — GROUCHO (PROCESS)

Mounted on a motorcycle, bent over the handlebars, doing a thousand miles an hour on the clouds. His ever-present cigar clamped between his teeth, he shoots a roguish look at the CAMERA and flexes his eyebrows in the typical Groucho manner. His bike is reminiscent of the earthbound motorcycle cops' vehicle, bedecked with the various accoutrements, including two-way radio. Over this the titles continue.

and

GROUCHO MARX
as
DEPUTY SERAPH

As the titles end the action continues.

FULL SHOT — CLOUD

Supporting Chico, Harpo and their instruments. They are still playing the hot tune. Faintly, the siren is HEARD. Chico stoops playing, looks off, reacts.

                    CHICO
                  (to Harpo)
        Hey, Harpo! Pipe down — here comes the
        chief.

Harpo stops, looks off.

HIS POV (PROCESS)

Groucho speeding along on his motorcycle. He is now doing a handstand on the handlebars. He rights himself, stands on the saddle in a nonchalant pose, raises one foot and poses.

BACK TO SCENE

                    CHICO
                  (to Harpo)
          Get rid of your harp.

Harpo nods understanding, blows at the harp and it *vanishes*. Chico runs his finger down the keyboard of the piano in his characteristic arpeggio, slays it with a final pistol shot and it, too, *disappears*. They are quite pleased with themselves.

                    CHICO
        Hey, you don't look like no angel. Disguise
        yourself!

Harpo makes the celebrated Harpo "FACE."

                    CHICO
          No! Your halo! Put on your *halo*!

Harpo regards him blankly, toots horn.

                    CHICO
                (waving his hands)
          Your halo. Halo!
                (his hand is extended)
          Halo!

With which, Harpo, comprehending completely, shakes his hand vigorously at the same time whistling "Hello"! "Pleased to meet you."

>   CHICO
> Not hello! Halo. Watch.

He makes a gesture into space and a halo appears over his head where it remains suspended magically in the air.

>   CHICO
> Hurry up — he's coming. I'll get the Good
> Book.

Harpo reaches into the atmosphere and a halo materializes in his hand. He turns his triumphant smile to Chico who nods encouragingly, then Harpo promptly beings to *eat the halo*.

>   WIDER ANGLE

As Groucho roars into the scene on his motorcycle. He brakes it violently, then regards Chico and Harpo who stand there the picture of angelic innocence, Harpo still munching on his halo.

>   GROUCHO
>   (shaking his head)
> Well I'd like to talk to you some
> more — but now it's time to play "I wish I
> was dead!"
>   (turns to CAMERA)
> Say the secret word and you can have
> them both.
>   (to Chico)
> Well, whose life did you foul up
> yesterday?

>   CHICO
> Nobody, boss. We pulled the right strings
> and everybody she's happy.

                    GROUCHO
         She is, eh?

                     CHICO
         Here's the report.

He hands Groucho the Good Book. Harpo moves in to peer over Groucho's shoulder.

                    GROUCHO
                (glancing at page)
         Hmm. So you got that young Englishman
         knighted for his operations in the stock
         market.

                     CHICO
           (as Harpo nods, violently happy)
         Goo, eh boss?

                    GROUCHO
         Perfect. Except it was the black
         market — and he should have been
         indicated — not knighted.

                     CHICO
                    (shrugs)
         Well, one swallow doesn't make a summer.

Harpo shrugs philosophically, too. Then they beam at each other and extend hands for a handshake. Harpo withdraws his hand and immediately hooks his thigh into Chico's grip. Chico knocks his leg away as Harpo screams with silent laughter. Suddenly there is a crackling NOISE from the motorcycle radio. The three angels become alert.

                     VOICE
                   (on filter)
         Attention all angels in the vicinity...and
         the Deputy Seraph.

> GROUCHO
> (into Mike)

Roger.

> CHICO
> (into Mike)

Chico.

Harpo blows his horn and mouths "Harpo" into mike.

> VOICE
> The French Riviera, between Cannes and Monte Carlo on the east side of the street — a four-oh-nine.

All three look down earthward.

CUT TO:

INT, HOTEL SUITE — MED. SHOT — DAY

A beautiful girl walks into the room. She adjusts some flowers in a vase.

> VOICE (cont'd)
> This confused female, blond, beautiful, aged twenty-three —

CUT TO:

INT. FURNISHED ROOM

In a typical French pension. A young man labors over some lead sheets. He is finishing a piano concerto.

> VOICE
> — and this male American, twenty-seven, six-two-one-seventy-four, must be married to each other by eight thirty tonight. Names, Linda Pavane and Paul MacDowell.

FULL SHOT—CLOUD

Harpo, Chico and Groucho look at each other with satisfaction indicating there is no problem. Groucho looks at his wristwatch. Chico pulls out a heavy railroad timepiece on a thick chain, pulls out a sundial, complete with pedestal. As he studies it for a shadow the VOICE continues.

      VOICE
 Proceed with caution. MacDowell is a
 confirmed woman-hater—

All three react.

          CUT TO:

INT. HOTEL SUITE

Linda goes to the door, opens it. Andre Lazar enters, they embrace passionately and he slips an engagement ring on her finger.

      VOICE
    (over action)
 Linda is engaged to somebody else—

ANGEL WIDENS

To include a partially opened door thru which we seen another room in the suite. The CAMERA DOLLIES past the embracing couple to show CESAR PAVANE, the world's greatest piano virtuoso at the grand piano, fingering the keys, moodily.

>   VOICES
> —and her uncle and guardian will not
> permit her to marry anybody!

Pavane brings both hands down on the keys with a crash in a fit of temper.

FULL SHOT CLOUD

Groucho shakes his head.

>   VOICE
>   That is all.

>   GROUCHO
>   (to the others)
>   Well, you heard him. Now if the two of you will
>   apply yourselves with your customary diligence
>   you should be able to screw this one up in
>   record time.

He leaps astride his motorcycle, revs it up.

>   CHICO
>   Leave it to us, boss. We get them married
>   before you can say Robinson Crusoe.

Harpo is already hugging and kissing Chico to show how quickly they will have the couple married.

>   GROUCHO
>   Now, you know what they mean by Divine
>   Providence.

He flicks his cigar and a great cloud of white ash falls in a shower towards the earth.

>   GROUCHO
> There. That's the first time they ever had
> snow in Bali-Bali.

All three suddenly react.

>   GROUCHO
>   (a take)
>   Bali-Bali!

They instantly strain their eyes towards the earth, Harpo whipping out a pair of binoculars. As they enjoy the native produce we

FADE OUT

FADE IN:

MONTAGE—FRENCH RIVIERA—DAY (STOCK)

The landscape and beaches of the French Riviera are established.

LONG SHOT—EXT. CASINO—DAY (STOCK)

A plush gambling casino.

DISSOLVE THRU:

FULL SHOT—INT. CASINO

CAMERA SWEEPS the interior of the richly-appointed casino, with the well-dressed crowd gathered around the tables.

FULL SHOT—AT DOOR

There is a slight stir at the door...a person of some importance is entering. The patrons fall back as a huge, bearded man enters, followed by his retinue. This is Cesar Pavane, the greatest living master of the piano. Pavane is dressed in the traditional grand manner, with little concession to modernity. His retinue consists of DR. SCHLAMM, a thin, all-knowing Viennese psychiatrist; PLANCHER, the harassed

French manager of the maestro; and BENSON, Don Diego's English valet.

Pavane presses forward quickly, CAMERA TRAVELING with him. He is oblivious to the stares of the other patrons, some of whom are pointing out the great pianist to their companions. The maestro heads straight for the roulette table, with the other players falling back before him as jackals upon the entrance of the lion.

AT TABLE

The CROUPIER bows as Pavane seats himself at the table, with the chair being pulled out for him by the valet. Wordlessly — following a familiar routine — Pavane signals for five stacks of chips. They are placed in front of him. He then pulls out and consults a small black notebook, which evidently contains his system of play.

Having made his selection, the maestro flexes his fingers — an instinctive gesture. He then gives a slight signal to the croupier, who puts the ball into action.

                          CROUPIER
            Faites vos jeux, monsieur... faites vous jeux.

Pavane is now ready to perform the final, climactic gesture. The delicate and sensitive fingers of the great pianist push out one of his stacks of chips.

                          PAVANE
            Quatorze.

                          CROUPIER
            Quatorze. Rien ne vas plus, rien ne va plus.

Pavane leans forward, watching the spinning wheel. The valet takes out notebook and pencil... his function is to record the run of the wheel.

CLOSE SHOT — WHEEL

The ball comes to rest. It settles in fifteen.

AT TABLE

> CROUPIER
> Quinze! Noir, impair!

Pavane quickly pushes out two stacks of the remaining four.

> PAVANE
> Quatorze!

> CROUPIER
> (spinning bell)
> Quatorze. Rien ne vas plus, rein ne vas plus.

Pavane leans forward with increased intensity. His manager looks on worriedly, as if he would like to restrain the maestro. Dr. Schlamm studies Pavane clinically. The ball clicks into a slot.

> CROUPIER
> Dix-huit! Rouge, pair!

Pavane takes a breath. The manager steps forward, but Pavane brushes him off with a wave of the hand. He pushes out his remaining two stacks.

> PAVANE
> Quatorze!

> CROUPIER
> (apinning ball)
> Quatorze. Rien ne vas plus, rien ne vas plus.

As Pavane leans forward, the sweat can be seen starting from his brow. We begin to see him now as the compulsive gambler, in whom the moment of play has replaced food, women ... even his music. The ball clicks into place.

> CROUPIER
> Vingt-et-un! Noir, impair!

Pavane leans back heavily in his chair. A sigh escapes the watching crowd. Pavane then straightens, and signals the croupier.

> PAVANE
> *Ten* stacks.

Plancher, the manager, can no longer hold back. He bends to talk swiftly to Pavane.

> PLANCHER
> But Maestro, you promised! One million francs, no more!

> PAVANE
> Plancher. Are you manager of the world's one great pianist, or are you still a masseur in a Turkish bath? Stand back.

> PLANCHER
> But you have not practiced in weeks.

> PAVANE
> Let the others practice. They may become may equals... in another fifty years. Quatorze!

Pavane pushes out three stacks of chips. As the ball spins, CAMERA PULS BACK RAPIDLY, until we are looking at the PICTURE THROUGH A SMALL FRAME.

INT. OFFICE

The office of the casino owner, ANDRE LAZAR, a darkly handsome continental. From the small window where he has been watching the play, Andre goes rapidly to a phone on his desk, dialing a number.

> ANDRE
> Picard? Lazar. Two million francs on Halcyon, in the seventh race today... I will *have* the money for you, *all* of it!

He slams down the phone. The door opens, and LINDA PAVANE enters. Andre springs to his feet, erasing his frown.

                    ANDRE
Linda darling! And how delightful, in that dress!

                    LINDA
Thank you, Andre.

He goes quickly to her, hands and kissing her. She turns her cheek just slightly, taking his kiss on her cheek instead of her lips.

                    LINDA
Is my uncle here?

                    ANDRE
As always.

He leads her to the window, where she looks out. As she does so, Andre suddenly kisses the back of her neck, then takes her in a passionate embrace.

                    ANDRE
Marry me, dearest! Now! Tonight!

                    LINDA
You know I can't, Andre, without Uncle's consent. You know he controls my estate.

Andre lets her go.

                    ANDRE
           (a trace of sarcasm)
Ah! Of course. And your trip back to America last summer, alone? That was with his consent?

LINDA
I've told you! Whatever happened last summer is over ... finished!

ANDRE
Of course. Hen it is only uncle.

LINDA
He'll never agree.

Andre looks through the window, at the play.

ANDRE
No? I think, darling, that soon he will be more — understanding.

CUT TO:

ROULETTE TABLE — MED. SHOT

Pavane, furious at his luck with the wheel, has a large stake on the board. He leans forward heavily as the wheel turns, his brow moist.

CROUPIER
Dix-neuf! Noir, impair!

He rakes in Pavane's chips. The feverish maestro does not pause a moment.

PAVANE
Twenty stacks!

Plancher tries to reason with him.

PLANCHER
Maestro. Already you have lost almost ten thousand dollars!

PAVANE
Back to your steam room, Plancher! One turn of the wheel, and I am even!

> (to Croupier)
> Four stacks, Quatorze!

In despair, Plancher turns to Dr. Schlamm, and draws him a few steps away from the table.

> PLANCHER
> He has gone made for the wheel! You
> are his analyst! Can you do nothing, Dr.
> Schlamm?

> SCHLAMM
> It is common. Schweinhundt's Mania...I
> could cure this personality disturbance in
> five minutes.

> PLANCHER
> Then why do you not?

> SCHLAMM
> I can not get him away from the wheel.

There is a disturbance as a young American forces his way through the crowd, with several casino employees restraining him. He is demanding to see Pavane. Plancher goes over, dismissing the casino men.

> PLANCHER
> I shall handle this.
> (to the American)
> you have business with...?
> (breaks off)
> Oh. It is you.

Plancher looks with distaste at the American, PAUL MacDOWELL. He is a handsome, intense young man, not notably well dressed but with a certain artistic flair. He is carrying in his hand the sheets of a musical composition.

> PAUL
> Get out of the way, Plancher.

The American is grimly determined. Plancher decides to be conciliatory.

> PLANCHER
> But Monsieur MacDowell... you cannot see the Maestro now. He is losing... the worst possible time.

> MACDOWEL
> (bursting out)
> I can't see him because he's gambling! I can't see him because he's eating! I can't see him because he's practicing! When can I see him?

> PLANCHER
> If you will just give your concerto to me...

He holds out his hand for the music, but MacDowell draws back...

> MACDOWELL
> On, no! Give my only copy to you? I'll give it to him... no one else!

He pushes past Plancher. CAMERA PANS WITH Mac Dowell to the table, where Pavane has six stacks riding on quatorze.

> CROUPIER
> Douze! Rouge, pair!

Pavane thumps his notebook on the table in a rage.

> PAVANE
> It is this wheel! My system could not be wrong! It is infallible — No, Benson?

> BENSON
> (doubtfully)
> Well, in the apartment, sir...

> PAVANE
> (roars)
> Silence! It must be quatorze! Now! Now!

Pavane ignores him, lost in the fever of the play.

> PAUL
> Monsieur Pavane, I have followed you all over Europe, trying to get my music to you.

> PAVANE
> (studying book)
> Go away.

Plancher pulls at Paul's sleeve, but the American shakes him off.

> PAUL
> All over Europe, and you can't give me two minutes!

Pavane turns and looks at him for the first time.

> PAVANE
> Why should I?

> PAUL
> Because my concerto may be just what you need, because I just might have talent!

> PAVANE
> It is most unlikely,

He turns back to the table, prepared to make his wager.

> PAVANE
> Croupier...

The ball clicks into the slot.

> CROUPIER
> (droning)
> Quatorze, fourteen!

Pavane is stunned.

> PAVANE
> Quatorze?... And I did not bet!

Paul is unaware of what he has done.

> PAUL
> Maestro... please! My concerto —

Pavane rises, icy calm.

> PAVANE
> Your concerto? Of course.

He takes it from him, and methodically tears it in shreds. Paul watches wordlessly as the Maestro does the job, and the pieces flutter to the floor.

Pavane storms out, as Paul bends down to gather up the pieces.

AT DOOR

Lazar emerges from his office, followed by Linda, as Pavane passes. He does not see them, blind with rage. A WOMAN, an obvious American tourist, approaches him with a piece of paper.

> TOURIST
> Oh, Maestro! Would you be good enough
> to sign this for my nephew back in Iowa
> City? He just adores your...

Wordlessly, Pavane strikes the paper out of her hands with his cane, and strides on.

CUT TO:

THE CLOUD

Chico and Harpo are looking down.

> CHICO
> Well, the first thing we gotta do is split up
> that pair... That's your job, Harpo.

Harpo shakes his head and hides behind Chico.

> CHICO
> It's easy! Don't be scared. All you gotta
> do is crawl inside of that sneaky feller
> and — you know! Go do your stuff.

A light dawns on Harpo's face! He looks down their vanishes. Chico smiles.

CUT TO:

INT. CASINO—AT DOOR

Lazar and Linda are still standing near the door of the casino, looking in the direction of Pavane's exit.

       ANDRE
       (smugly)
  I have a feeling, darling, that your uncle's
  consent is near. Very near.

       LINDA
  I'll see you at dinner, Andre.

She holds out her hand, in farewell. Andre is suddenly motionless, staring.

HIS PV

Harpo's horn-stick is floating toward him.

ANDRE AND LINDA

Linda suddenly finds herself holding Andre's leg in her outstretched arm. The stick has floated into Andre's hand. He has now become inhabited with Harpo's spirit.

       LINDA
  Andre!

She slaps his leg away.

Andre turns TO CAMERA, making the "HARPO FACE". At this moment, a generously endowed blonde strolls by in a beach outfit, wearing a loose skirt and jacket over her swimming bra and shorts. Andre honks. The blonde looks back, and sees him coming for her. She takes off at a run. Andre follows, honking and whistling. As al the patrons stare, a mad chase develops, with Andre pursuing the fleeing blonde around and over gaming tables, behind pillars, and in and out the doors of the terrace. The is INTERCUT WITH REACTIONS SHOTS of Linda and of the patrons. The blonde disappears to the terrace, closely pursued. There is a SHRIEK, and the emerges minus her jacket. Later, the business is repeated, with the skirt being lost. When she is down to swimming trunks and bra, the chase goes by Linda. Timing her swing well, she catches Andre in full flight with an open-handed blow to the cheek. He goes down, staring up at her dazed as she stalks off.

WIPE TO:

THE CLOUD

Chico stands, looking down and laughing. Suddenly, Harpo materializes beside him sitting on the floor. He holds a hand to his face in mock pain. Chico helps him to his feet and they laugh and congratulate each other.

ANOTHER CLOUD

MED SHOT—GROUCHO

On his motorcycle. He is at a standstill, looking down. He dismounts, obviously disapproving of what has happened, and lopes across the cloud using his famous crouching walk.

GROUCHO
(to CAMERA)
A fine pair of idiots! Making a woman
jealous to bust up a romance hasn't
worked for as long as my brother
Gummo. The idea is to concentrate on
the boy.

He reaches out his hand and a phone magically materializes in it. He acts somewhat startled as he lifts the receiver.

GROUCHO
I wonder how they do that?... Hello—

DISSOLVE:

HOTEL CORRIDOR—DAY

The door of Pavane's suite is being barred by Plancher, who is arguing violently with Paul MacDowell. The young American has his damaged but patched music manuscript in his hand.

> PAUL
> But I tell you, he called! He wanted to see me!

> PLANCHER
> It is impossible. The Maestro hates you. Besides he never uses the telephone.

> PAUL
> That's a lie! Nobody could imitate his voice!

CUT TO:

CLOSE SHOT—GROUCHO—He winks and pats the phone then vanishes.

BACK TO SCENE:

Plancher comes out, closing the door behind him.

> PLANCHER
> Monsieur MacDowell. I too would like Pavane to have your concerto. I have seen it, I know its worth. But at this time, no. We have greater problems with the maestro... far greater problems.

> PAUL
> (bewildered)
> But why did he send for me?

> PLANCHER
> He did not. Believe me.

Plancher starts back insider. Paul turns to go, bumping directly into a WAITER who is carrying a huge tray of food. Miraculously, the tray remains balanced in mid-air and the waiter brushes off Paul while apologizing in voluble French. Both Plancher and Paul spot the suspended tray at the same time — or THINK they do. The waiter with a lightning movement has his hand under it again. They react, in doubt as to what they DID see. Plancher holds the door open for the waiter, who goes in. Paul starts down the hallway, then realizes he does not have his manuscript. He searches for it in his pockets, looking around on the floor at the same time. He glances at the closed door of Pavane's suite, wondering.

INSIDE SUITE

Pavane, assisted by Benson, is feverishly plotting the run of a roulette wheel he has set up on a table. Benson jots the numbers down as Pavane spins the wheel. Plancher and Schlamm are also present. The waiter is quickly and professionally preparing a table with the food he has brought in.

                    PAVANE
        Quatorze! Again quatorze! Always the
        second section! My system is infallible! ...
        then why does it fail?

Benson consults the book.

                    BENSON
        Begging your pardon, sir, I just notice one
        small weakness, sir.

                    PAVANE
        What is that? What is that?

                    BENSON
        It doesn't work when you plan for money
        Pavane collapses, waving his hands
        weakly.

                    PAVANE
        Why? Why? Plancher steps forward.

PLANCHER
Maestro. Your good is ready.

PAVANE
In the hotel room, I am powerful, invincible! In the casino... they laugh at me.

PLANCHER
(worriedly)
But you must eat, Maestro!

PAVANE
(abject)
They laugh at me.

PLANCHER
(to Schlamm)
Doctor...

SCHLAMM
(an aside)
It is nothing — a morbid desire to lose face — Unterwesche's Syndrome...

Dr. Schlamm steps forward.

SCHLAMM
You remember, Don Diego, the days of your strength, your glory?

PAVANE
I remember, yes.

SCHLAMM
You remember how you would eat?... great quantities of food?

Pavane begins to come alive.

                    PAVANE
          Quantities, yes. Great quantities

                    SCHLAMM
          And nobody has laughed because you
          were strong... very strong!

Pavane rises, going over to the table.

                    PAVANE
          I shall eat! And I shall be strong again!
          And powerful! And filled with glory!

Pavane lifts the cover of one of the dishes, sniffing with great relish.

CLOSE SHOT—DISH

The patched manuscript is resting on the plate.

BACK TO SCENE

                    PAVANE
                (almost screaming)
          What is this? What is this?

THE WAITER

He looks INTO CAMERA, flexes his eyebrows, then takes a lighted cigar out of the air and taps some ashes on Pavane's head, leaving with the Groucho walk.

CORRIDOR

Paul approaches the waiter, who is coming out the door.

                    PAUL
          Pardon. But have you seen some music?
          Une manuscript de musique?

The waiter gestures toward the door of the suite, then wiggles his eyebrows while indicating with another gesture that Paul is in like Flynn. He then lopes down the corridor in the Groucho walk, as Paul stares after him. Paul then shrugs, approaches the door and goes in.

INSIDE SUITE

As Paul enters, Pavane is standing, livid. He holds the offending manuscript in both hands.

      PAVANE
     (seeing Paul)
 Aha! You!

He starts tearing the manuscript into shreds. Paul starts for him.

      PAUL
 Why, you...!

He is hastily intercepted by Benson, Plancher, and Schlamm. Still trying to get at Pavane, who continues tearing the music with relish, Paul is propelled through the door and out.

OUTSIDE DOOR

Lying on the floor outside the door, Paul is showered with the scraps of his music, thrown by Pavane. The door slams shut.

          CUT TO:

THE CLOUD

Chico and Harpo are looking down. Groucho, still with his waiter's napkin over his arm, materializes alongside of them. He, too, looks down.

      GROUCHO
 Well, you can't win 'em all.

      CHICO
 Look. He's a piano player, I'm a piano
 player. I fix him.

Chico POPS OUT of the picture. Groucho and Harpo look down. Groucho then looks INTO CAMERA.

> GROUCHO
> He's not bright, but he'sscrupulously dishonest

He dematerializes, leaving Harpo.

DISSOLVE:

INT. SUITE

It is a few moments later. Pavane is again seated at the table, which is now loaded with food. Plancher and Schlamm watch him anxiously. He starts to attack the food with gusto.

> PAVANE
> I shall eat, I shall again be strong, I shall...

With his fork on its way to his mouth, he stops.

> PLANCHER
> What is it?

Pavane puts down the fork

> PAVANE
> At the casino. They are laughing at me.

> PLANCHER
> But you must eat, so you can practice!
> Your big concert of the season is tonight,
> and you have not been ear you piano!

Pavane merely makes a waving, defeated motion with his hands. Schlamm takes over.

> SCHLAMM
> But they do not laugh, do they, when you sit down at your piano?

                    PAVANE
Laugh? Never!

                    SCHLAMM
At the piano you feel secure, capable.

                    PAVANE
Secure, yes!

He rises, going toward the piano.

                    SCHLAMM
You are powerful... you fear nothing.

Pavane sits down, striking the keys powerfully.

                    PAVANE
There is power! It flows from my fingers.
Cesar Pavane fears nothing!

He plows into a powerful passage, attacking with fury. Suddenly, he stares.

HIS POV

Chico's hat is floating toward him.

CLOSE SHOT—PAVANE

He looks around, but the others have seen nothing. He passes a hand over his face, and resumes playing. Now the Chico hat is on his head, and he is playing the CHICO THEME. (He has now become host for Chico's spirit and his actions well parallel Chico's.)

TWO SHOT—SCHLAMM AND PLANCHER

They stare at each other.

CLOSE SHOT—KEYBOARD

Pavane's fingers are playing in the Chico manner, shooting the keys.

BACK TO SCENE

Plancher and Schlamm stare at Pavane, who has his back to them, at the piano. He continues to shoot the keys with his finger.

>PLANCHER
>Maestro! What are you doing? That tune, that atrocious technique!

HEAD SHOT—PAVANE

He continues to play, but his expression is bewildered, frightened.

>PAVANE
>(Italian dialect)
>Im'a no canna help it!

AT PIANO

Schlamm and Plancher come quickly to PAVANE, to lead him away from the piano.

> PLANCHER
> You must lie down, Maestro. You must
> rest. You must...

They are now puling at him, but he resists, still playing. At a signal from Schlamm, Benson comes over and helps them pull. The piano bench overturns, and al four end up in a tangle on the floor.

CUT TO:

THE CLOUD

Harpo is looking down, Chico materializes on the cloud, picks himself up, rubbing his posterior. Harpo helps him to his feet, rubs too.

CUT TO:

INT. SUITE

Schlamm and Plancher are helping Pavane to a couch. They get him onto the couch, where he lies still, breathing heavily and obviously shaken.

> PAVANE
> What... what happened? I was playing
> with power, without fear, and then...

> SCHLAMM
> Yes? And then?

> PAVANE
> My hands, I lost the control of my hands!

He waves them about, to show what happened. Schlamm takes them, and folds them firmly but gently on Pavane's expansive stomach.

SCHLAMM
Ah. Now we begin to see…

PLANCHER
(anxiously)
What is it? Can he still play the concert?

Schlamm waves him to silence.

SCHLAMM
And how did you feel, Monsieur Pavane, when you lost control of your hands?

PAVANE
I was… without strength. As a small boy.

SCHLAMM
A small boy. Did you feel that you had lost control of your hands because you had been doing bad things with those hands?

PAVANE
Ho. Yes. I do not know.

SCHLAMM
You can remember if you try, Cesar Pavane. What did you do with those hands? Was there blood on them? Were they red from blood?

Pavane suddenly bounces up off the couch.

PAVANE
That is it! Red! I shall not play fourteen, I shall play red! Only rouge! Benson! Come!

Grabbing his stick and black book, Pavane goes rapidly across the room and out the door. Benson gathers up Pavane's hat and gloves, and follows. Schlamm turns to Plancher.

> SCHLAMM
> A very interesting case... Morbid
> guilt complex, coupled with Flagel's
> Psychosis... easy to cure.

Plancher glares at him, then starts after Pavane.

CUT TO:

INT. PENSION—DAY

A small, poorly furnished room where Paul has been lodging. He is now furiously throwing his few belongings into a suitcase. Madame Tusseaux, his ancient French landlady, watches anxiously.

> TUSSEAUX
> Monsieur is leaving? Monsieur does not
> enjoy the Riviera?

> PAUL
> Monsieur is through! Fed up!

> TUSSEAUX
> I do not understand the fed up.

> PAUL
> Madame Tusseaux. I have taken months
> out of my life to get my concerto to one
> man... a man with the exquisite sensitivity
> of a crocodile.

> TUSSEAUX
> Ah. Le Croc.

> PAUL
> I have run out of time, I have run out of
> money. I am going home, to spend the
> rest of my life on an onion farm!

He closes his suitcase viciously. Madame Tusseaux points to a picture on the bureau.

> TUSSEAUX
> Monsieur has forgotten the beautiful lady

Paul goes over and picks up the photograph.

INSERT—PHOTO

A picture of Linda, inscribed, "To Paul, with all my love forever. Linda."

BACK TO SCENE

> PAUL
> (bitterly)
> Monsieur is also fed up with the beautiful lady.

He puts the photo face down on the bureau, and picks up his suitcase.

> TUSSEAUX
> Monsieur is also fed up with the beautiful lady.

He puts the photo face down on the bureau, and picks up his suitcase.

> TUSSEAUX
> Monsieur. A few times in the past I have had lodgers with the fed ups. For them, I have a lucky thousand franc note.

She rummages in her clothing, and comes up with a battered note

> TUSSEAUX
> Take it to the casino, Monsieur Paul. Take it. It may bring you riches.

> PAUL
> Madame Tusseaux, I thank you. But all I need is my ticket home. I'll be sailing at seven this evening.

He has pulled out his ticket to make sure he has it. He replaces it in his pocket, and starts to leave.

CUT TO:

THE CLOUD

Chico, Harpo, and Groucho are looking down.

> CHICO
> Hey! Why's he goin' sailing at seven when he's gotta get married at eight-thirty?

> GROUCHO
> Chico, once again your native intelligence has gone to the heart of the problem. We'd better detain him.

He reaches out his hand, and a phone magically appears in it.

DISSOLVE:

INT. CASINO—DAY

Pavane is at the roulette table, with Benson behind him. Pavane is ignoring the commotion going on a short distance away, where Plancher and Schlamm are restraining a furious Paul.

CLOSER ANGLE—PAUL, PLANCHER, SCHLAMM

> PAUL
> But he called me again! On the telephone!

> PLANCHER
> No, no, no. Impossible!

PAUL
(firmly)
He called me to come to the casino! Said he wanted to discuss my concerto!

SCHLAMM
Young man. These delusions of yours...

PAUL
Stop saying that! I was on my way to the boat. I have no more time. I have no more money. And then he called me!

SCHLAMM
Ah. An obvious wish-fulfillment daydream. Have you experienced other fantasies of this...

PAUL
(cutting in)
All right! If the Maestro doesn't want to talk to me, he doesn't want to talk to me. But left *him* tell me!

He struggles to get past them. A CASINO OFFICIAL comes up.

OFFICIAL
(to Paul)
Monsieur. It is not permitted to annoy the players.

PAUL
You can't keep me away from the table! The wheel is open to the public, isn't it?

OFFICIAL
Only for players, Monsieur.

> PLANCHER
> And he has no money!

Plancher and Schlamm grab Paul as he makes another attempt to get by them. He wrestles free, and turns to bump forcibly into a large, dignified DOWAGER with abundant blond curls. Paul goes down. The casino official brushed off the woman, apologizing.

> OFFICIAL
> A thousand pardons, Madame. We regret
> exceedingly that...

The official's back is TO CAMERA. The dowager suddenly makes the Harpo face at him. He recoils. The dowager sails off, accompanied by HONKING SOUNDS. The official stares after her, shakes his head to clear it, then turns to Paul.

> OFFICIAL
> If you have no money, Monsieur, I shall
> have to request that you do not go to the
> tables.

Paul, who is brushing himself off, feels something in his coat pocket, and pulls it out. It I s a huge roll of franc notes.

> PLANCHER
> Where did you get that?

> PAUL
> (doubtfully)
> From... from my landlady. I think.
> (going forward)
> One side, Messieurs.

He strides to the table, CAMERA FOLLOWING.

AT TABLE

Pavane looks up in anger as Paul comes to the table.

                    PAUL
Did you phone me?

                    PAVANE
I? You are mad!
          (to the official)
Remove him.

                    OFFICIAL
          (apologetically)
The play is public, Maestro.

Paul turns to the croupier, with a flourish.

                    PAUL
One chip, please.

He peels a note from his roll, and receives his chip. Pavane glares at him, and he smiles pleasantly back. The croupier spins the wheel.

                    CROUPIER
Faites vos jeux, Messieurs. Place your bets.

                    PAUL
I'll wait for him.

Trying to ignore Paul, Pavane pushes out a large pile of chips.

                    PAVANE
Red!

                    PAUL
Black.

He places his one chip. Pavane glares at him as the wheel spins. The ball clicks into the slot.

                    CROUPIER
Seven, black!

He rakes in Pavane's chips, and pays off Paul, who prudently drags down one chip. He spins the wheel again.

> CROUPIER
> Place your bets, Messieurs. Faites vox jeux.

Pavane pushes out an even larger pile of chips.

> PAVANE
> Red

> PAUL
> (pleasantly)
> Black.

Behind Pavane, Benson slips away. The ball spins.

CLOSE SHOT—TABLE

By themselves, Pavane's chips move from the red to the black. Paul's one chip moves from the black to the red.

AT TABLE

Pavane stares at the moving chips, then holds up his hands and looks at them, not certain if he has lost control again. The ball stops.

> CROUPIER
> Ten, red!

He takes Pavane's chips, and pays Paul.

> PAVANE
> But the chips! They moved! They...

He breaks off, not certain of his ground. He then plunges.

> PAVANE
> Twenty stacks! And all on the red!

                        PAUL
        One on black.

He places his one chip.

                                            CUT TO:

ANDRE'S OFFICE

Andre turns from the lookout window as Benson slips in the door.

                        ANDRE
        You have it, Benson?

He holds out his hand.

                        BENSON
        Not that you wouldn't be the soul of
        honesty, sir but I'd prefer the monetary
        settlement... in advance.

Lazar gives him a look, then goes to his desk and takes out a stack of bank notes, which he throws down on the desk. Benson picks them up, leafs through to count them, and then takes some papers from an inside pocket. He drops them on the desk, where Andre takes them up quickly.

                    BENSON
        There you are, sir but if I didn't need the
        money, I'd turn the nasty old walrus in
        to the coppers, I would! He's a common
        thief.

Andre goes to the window, smiling.

                    ANDRE
        Careful how you talk, Benson... I'm
        practically one of the family.

                                    CUT TO:

AT TABLE

The croupier has just place Pavane's twenty stacks on the red, and spins the ball. Pavane watches tensely.

                    CROUPIER
        Rien ne vas plus, rien ne vas plus.

Pavane watches the ball as it turns, as if his life depended on it. The ball slows, Pavane following it with his head.

CLOSE SHOT—WHEEL

About to come to rest, the ball begins to bounce.

CLOSE SHOT—PAVANE

Amazed, he follows it up and down with his head. It bounces higher and higher.

TABLE

All are looking on in amazement.

From the motion of Pavane's head, the ball is now bouncing lower.

>PAVANE
>Ah. It is bouncing in … in … Red!

CLOSE SHOT—WHEEL

The ball has come to rest in Red. Just as Pavane speaks, it takes one last bounce, to the next slot.

AT TABLE

>CROUPIER
>Twenty, black!

>PAVANE
>It could not be!

>PAUL
>(carefully)
>Well, that's the way the ball bounces.

>PAVANE
>Forty more stacks!

The croupier catches a signal from the office.

>CROUPIER
>The manager would like to see you in his office, Monsieur Pavane.

>PAVANE
>I shall return!

CUT TO:

THE CLOUD

Harpo and Chico are looking down, killing themselves with laughter.

Harpo imitates the bouncing ball, and Chico joins him. Together they do somersaults, high leaps, layouts, dives and returns, until they finally collapse. (Trampoline — Doubles)

CUT TO:

ANDRE'S OFFICE

Andre turns from the window as Pavane storms in.

> PAVANE
> You deny me credit? Cesar Pavane, who has lost millions?

> ANDRE
> Yes I am overextended.
> (as Cesar reacts)
> You have the wheel, I have the horses. We are both overextended.

Pavane thumps the desk with his cane.

> PAVANE
> My concert tonight is sold out! I will wager it!

> ANDRE
> You already have. Fortunately, my fiancée still has enough for us both.

> PAVANE
> My niece marry a gambler? Never!

> ANDRE
> Then read this. Proof... that you have embezzled half of Linda's fortune, and thrown it away on the wheel.

He throws he papers at Pavane, who stares at them, glassy-eyed.

                    PAVANE
                    (hoarsely)
        You are a sneak!

                    ANDRE
        Linda will be here any minute. Have we
        reached on understanding... Uncle?

                                            CUT TO:

OUTSIDE OFFICE

Linda is entering, her hand on the door, She stops, staring.

HER PV

Paul is walking toward her. He stops, seeing her.

PAUL AND LINDA

There is a physical shock as they recognize each other. They are about to speak, and then do not. Linda enters the office, and Paul goes on.

INT. OFFICE

Linda enters, still shocked over seeking Paul. Pavane has made his decision.

                    PAVANE
        My dear, I congratulate you. I have just
        given your hand in marriage to this
        loathsome toad.

He stalks out. Linda is unable to digest what is going on.

                    LINDA
        Andre! What...?

                    ANDRE
        I charmed him. We'll be married tonight,
        right after the concert. Happy, darling?

Linda looks anything but happy.

CUT TO:

THE CLOUD

Chico and Harpo are still rolling with laughter over the bouncing bal. Groucho is looking down, sober. He motions for them to look down. They do, sobering.

          GROUCHO
          (accusingly)
Well?

          CHICO
          (shrugs)
Well, you can't make as omelet without breaking eggs.

          GROUCHO
Breaking eggs, eh?

He reaches out and magically his hands are full of eggs. As he advances menacingly on Chico and Harpo we

DISSOLVE:

FULL SHOT —INT. CASINO BAR —DAY

The bar is filled with glamorous Riviera types. CAMERA MOVES IN on Linda and Andre, seated a little distance from the other patrons.

          LINDA
But Andre... how can we be married this evening? I — I have hundreds of things to do!

          ANDRE
I know, darling. But there is one thing *I* must do. To assure myself that the — American episode is just that... only an episode.

                    LINDA
           How many times can I tell you?

                    ANDRE
           I prefer to see for myself.

Andre is looking off, over her shoulder.

ANOTHER ANGLE

Paul approaches the table, coming up behind Linda. He speaks to Andre, not recognizing Linda from the rear.

                    PAUL
           You wanted to see me?

Linda turns swiftly.

                    LINDA
           Paul!

They stare at each other a long moment. Andre bridges the gap by rising.

                    ANDRE
           Monsieur MacDowell, I believe you know
           my fiancee — Miss Pavane.

Linda turns to Andre.

                    LINDA
           Why did you do this, Andre?

                    ANDRE
                  (to Paul)
           You will sit down, Monsieur?

                    PAUL
           No thanks.

ANDRE
As you wish.
(to Linda)
Doubtless it would be more American, darling, to preserve a gentlemanly silence about your past amour... so that we would have something to quarrel about after our marriage, Being European, I prefer to dispose of the matter now.
(bowing)
I have business in my office. I leave you to make your farewells.

He goes off. Paul drops into a chair.

PAUL
What do I say? Congratulations? When does it take place?

LINDA
Andre wants it tonight. After my uncle's concert.

PAUL
I thought he wouldn't let you marry *anybody*. At least, that's what you told *me*.

LINDA
It was true!
(beat)
But he suddenly consented, to Andre. I don't know why.

PAUL
I hope you'll be ecstatically happy. I wouldn't trust him with yesterday's paper, but may be that's just the way he looks.

LINDA
Andre is a very handsome man!

PAUL
Yeah.
(rising)
Well, I'd love to stay and catch the bridal bouquet, but I've got a boat to make.

Linda suddenly reaches out and takes his hand.

LINDA
Paul, why didn't you tell me you were in Europe? Why couldn't we have seen each other? Why not until too late?

Paul sits down again, speaking with intensity.

PAUL
Did you think I didn't want to? Did you think it was easy, being in Rome with you, Paris, London... yet keeping away from you?

LINDA
But why?

PAUL
(bitterly)
I was going to do it your way. All right... so your uncle wouldn't accept some poor American he didn't even know. I was going to force him to recognize my genius. Ha. Well, it all worked out just fine. Uncle can't see my concerto without making confetti of it, and you're marrying the man of Uncle's dreams.

> LINDA
> I though I'd never see you again.

> PAUL
> That's what you said you wanted. Just because I called your uncle an obnoxious, overbearing barrel of blubber.

> LINDA
> You didn't even know him then!

> PAUL
> (shouting)
> Well I do now, and I was too kind to him! And as for you...

WIDER ANGLE

Andre has come up, and is enjoying the quarrel.

> ANDRE
> Ah. You get on well together?

> PAUL
> How would you like a punch in the nose?

> LINDA
> You can't talk to him that way!

> PAUL
> (rising)
> No? Well, I just did! And the best of luck to you both... you'll need it!

> ANDRE
> (smoothly)
> And the best of luck to your concerto... which may also need it?

Paul looks about to hit Andre, but changes his mind and stalks off.

CUT TO:

THE CLOUD

Chico and Harpo are looking down anxiously. Groucho takes a peek, then starts to think.

> CHICO
> Hey! By eight-thirty we gotta get 'em married... and they hate each other!

> GROUCHO
> The best possible beginning.
> (thinking)
> I've got the solution. We've got to make Uncle holler "Uncle"!

DISSOLVE:
FULL SHOT — STAGE — DAY

A full orchestra is on stage, tuning up. Most of them are dressed casually for the rehearsal, but a few — including the CONDUCTOR — are already in evening clothes. Plancher is conferring anxiously with the conductor.

Although we do not hear their conversation, they are apparently waiting on Pavane. Plancher goes off into the wings, CAMERA PANNING with him.

IN WINGS

Pavane is reclining in a contour lounge, with Schlamm sitting beside him. Although the location is far from private, with stagehands and musicians passing by, it is the best Schlamm has been able to manage. He waves Plancher to silence as the letter comes on. Schlamm continues talking to Pavane.

> SCHLAMM
> And the gambling, Monsieur Pavane... do you understand why you gamble?

> PAVANE
> I do not understand by I *Lose!* Rouge, noir, noir, rouge... with only two choices, how can I always be wrong?

> SCHLAMM
> It is quite simple. Unconsciously, you wish to lose.

> PAVANE
> Fool! I wish to win!

> SCHLAMM
> (relentless)
> You wish to lose. It is a form of Coniff's Disease, or Cockamania.

> PLANCHER
> (anxiously)
> Maestro... Dr. Schlamm... the orchestra is waiting to rehearse.

Schlamm impatiently waves him off, continuing.

> SCHLAMM
> You wish to lose because you are punishing yourself for some hidden guilt.

> PAVANE
> I am punishing myself.
> (rejects this)
> No! It is bad luck, it is the way the ball bounces, it is... my hands.

Schlamm drives into the opening.

> SCHLAMM
> Ah. Your hands. You lost control of those guilty hands, as you did at the piano!

> PAVANE
> I was in perfect control at the Piano!
> (doubt again)
> But when I saw the pointy hat, I...

His fingers play in the air, in the Chico manner.

> SCHLAMM
> The pointy hat! Described by Wegerfarth... the childhood fear of the dunce cap!

> PAVANE
> I am not guilty! I have done nothing.

He continues to play in the air, shooting the keys.

> SCHLAMM
> (crescendo)
> You were shooting the piano keys, but the one you really wished to kill was... yourself.

> PAVANE
> No! No! No!
>   (stops playing, in the middle of a shot)
> That's right!

> SCHLAMM
> (climaxing)
> And now that you have faced your problem, Cesar Pavane, you will go to the piano, and play!

> PAVANE
> (rising)
> I shall go to my piano, and play!

He strides off, toward the stage.

FULL SHOT — STAGE

As Pavane strides to his piano, placed in front of the orchestra, the conductor tapes the stand with his baton. The orchestra comes to attention, and the conductor gives the downbeat. They launch into "_____."

AT PIANO

Pavane is playing brilliantly, with great power.

IN WINGS

Plancher and Schlamm are watching with gratification.

AT PIANO

Pavane is playing with his eyes closed, lost in the emotion of the music. He opens his eyes, and stares.

HIS PV

The pointy hat is floating toward him.

ORCHESTRA

They are tacit, with the piano taking the solo part. Suddenly, Pavane begins to play in the Chico manner, and wearing the Chico hat. The conductor, confused, gives an uncertain downbeat to the orchestra. Discords begin to develop.

IN WINGS

Plancher is staring in consternation.

> PLANCHER
> The madness again!

> SCHLAMM
> Entirely predictable. The Hocker
> Syndrome.

PLANCHER
You will give me no Hockers!... He is sick
in the head!

ORCHESTRA

Confusion now reigns, with Pavane still playing in the Chico manner.

HARPIST

He suddenly makes the Harpo face, INTO CAMERA. He then turns to the very attractive woman CELLIST, next to him. He honks, starting toward her. She flees.

ORCHESTRA

The Harpist is now chasing the Cellist through the orchestra, adding to the confusion.

CONDUCTOR

He is desperately trying to conduct, then suddenly stops and stares. A lighted cigar is floating toward him. He takes the cigar and puts it in his mouth, wiggling his eyebrows.

ORCHESTRA

The conductor is striding back and forth in the Groucho walk, as the Harpist continues to chase the Cellist. As the chase progresses, the Cellist loses some article of clothing each time she disappears in the wings and is chased out again. The Conductor flips cigar ashes into the instrument of the base horn player, and then goes to where Pavane is still playing in the Chico manner. He breaks his baton over Pavane's head. The pointy hat falls off, and Pavane shaken comes center stage, addressing the orchestra.

PAVANE
(mysteriously)
It is true! I am guilty! I am a thief! With
these hands
(holding up hands)

> I have stolen from my niece! I have given
> her in marriage to a fortune hunter, a
> blackmailer! There will be no concert... I
> must stop the wedding!

During his speech, the conductor, harpist, and cellist continue to pass in front of him.

WINGS

Plancher and Schlamm rush on stage, to Pavane. Benson, who has been in the background, is on a phone.

> **BENSON**
> Mr. Lazar? There's a boat leaving in half
> an hour. If you want to marry the girl,
> you'd better be on it. Old Porky is up the
> flue.

DISSOLVE:

LONG SHORT —LINTER —NIGHT (STOCK)

An ocean liner, lights ablaze, going through calm seas.

DISSOLVE THRU:

INT. STATEROOM

A uniformed SHIP'S CAPTAIN is ready to perform the marriage ceremony. A PURSER and a pretty STEWARDESS are present to act as witnesses. Andre and Linda are off to one side of the room, holding a whispered conversation.

> **LINDA**
> But Andre.... I'm not sure. I'm not sure at all!

> **ANDRE**
> Either you go through with it, Linda, or
> your uncle will go to jail as an embezzler!

She stares at him, not knowing how to counter the threat.

CUT TO:

THE CLOUD

Harpo and Chico are looking down, fearfully. Groucho consults his watch.

> GROUCHO
> Eight twenty-nine. One of you better go down and break up that wedding. I'd go myself, but I'm subject to mal de mer.

> CHICO
> That's nothing, I get seasick!

They both look at Harpo, who pantomimes that he too gets seasick. Groucho shrugs, and stretches out his hand. The phone pops into it.

CUT TO:

INT. STATEROOM

> CAPTAIN
> And do you, Linda, take this man, Andre, for your lawful wedded husband?

The door bursts open, and Paul rushes in.

> PAUL
> All right — break it up!

All turn to the intruder. Paul goes straight to Andre, and without a word hits him on the chin. Andre folds, and lies still. Linda is shocked for a moment, then rushes to Paul's arms.

> LINDA
> Paul!

CAPTAIN
Would you mind explaining?

Paul explains over Linda's shoulder to the captain.

PAUL
She called me. Found out this fellow was a fortune hunter and blackmailer, and wanted me to save her.

Linda raises her head.

LINDA
(bewildered)
But Paul, I don't...

Paul pulls her head back to his cheat.

PAUL
Shah... it's all over.
(to the captain)
Would you mind going on with the ceremony, sir?

CAPTAIN
But the man's unconscious!

PAUL
Not him. Me.
(to Linda)
All right, honey?

Linda tearfully nods. The captain, with a shrug, takes up his book again.

CAPTAIN
Dearly beloved, we are gathered here...

CUT TO:

THE CLOUD

Chico and Harpo are dancing in happiness. Groucho checks his watch.

>   GROUCHO
>   (to Camera)
> On the nose! And I'll bet you thought
> we'd have trouble. Well, stick around.
> There's a few loose ends we have to tie off.

                                        FADE

EPILOGUE

FADE IN

EXT. CONCERT HALL NIGHT (STOCK)

                                 DISSOLVE THRU

FULL SHOT STAGE

A symphony orchestra is seated, the conductor has his baton poised, the downbeat is given, and to his musical introduction and thunderous applause Pavane strides majestically onto the stage.

TIGHT TWO SHORT LINDA AND PAUL

Somewhere in the darkened theatre. Their faces glow in anticipation.

>   LINDIA
> You'll hear it now for the firsttime,
> darling — your concerto —

Paul nods happily, too much in love to talk. They clasp hands.

STAGE PAVANE AT PIANO

With great technique, his hands flying over the keys with the lightness of thistledown, the Maestro launches into Paul's concerto. As the melody, though orchestrated symphonically, penetrates, we become aware he is playing the CHICO THEME. Enough to establish and then

DISSOLVE

THE CLOUD

Chico at the piano, Harpo at the harp, having picked up the concerto, are continuing dreamily. Groucho mounts his motorcycle, flicks the ash from his cigar, flexes his eyebrows at the camera, revs up the motor. The bike takes off leaving Groucho with the handlebars in his hands, magically suspended in a seated position as we

FADE OUT

THE END

JOAN OF ARKANSAS

Starring Joan Davis

ACT ONE

FADE IN:

AIR SHOT—WASHINGTON, D.C.—NIGTH (STOCK)

The principal government buildings should be identifiable.

MONTAGE—NIGHT

In a SERIES OF DISSOLVES We show the following:

A. The Treasury Building.

B. The while House.

C. The Pentagon.

D. Int. of large building.

E. A long deserted corridor.

F. A massive steel door.

These are all NIGHT SHOTS and are placed in such sequence as to produce a converging effect. Having reached the massive steel door the camera moves in a panel. The panel houses three small lights, the center one blinking incessantly and emitting an urgent "beep" SOUND at regular intervals.

WIPE:

3. INT. SLEEPING CHAMBER—NIGHT

It is a small, severely neat room, and despite the darkness the figure of a man can be distinguished in bed, asleep. The CAMERA MOVES RIGHT THRU the room and up to a small panel near the bedside. This panel is a duplicate of the one seen previously on the steel door. It has already begun to flash and BEEP. The sleeping figure is galvanized into action, and without turning on the light is speedily dressing.

DISSOLVE TO:

INT. SLEEPING CHAMBER — NIGHT .

The above action is repeated in every details, except that the man who dresses is a little slower and is apparently having trouble with one shoe.

DISSOLVE TO:

INT. SLEEPING CHAMBER — NIGHT

Once again we move into the room up to the panel with its blinking light and beckoning BEEP. The alerted figure dresses rapidly, and with great precision, as though going thru an oft-rehearsed routine.

DISSOLVE TO:

INT. GOVERNMENT BUILDING — CORRIDOR — NIGHT

A pair of militiamen stand guard, weapons at the ready, as the three men enter. We will only see their backs as the CAMERA FOLLOWS them on their long walk, but for practical purposes it is best to identify them now. The center figure is DR. CURTIS SHORT, a man of military bearing and determined step. His two colleagues are PROFESSOR HENRY NEWKIRK, he of the troublesome shoelace, and the younger but brilliant Dr. JOHN DOLAN. Whatever they show the sentries satisfies them and they are given free passage.

The **TITLES ARE NOW SUPERED** and continue over the following scene.

The three men hurry on towards the SOUND of the beep which is becoming louder and more insistent as they progress, the CAMERA FOLLOWING at a discreet distance. Rounding a turn in the corridor they are confronted by two more sentries, signs are flashed, and they would be on their way again, except professor Newkirk stops to tie his shoelace. Impatience can be seen even on the backs of the other two men. The job completed, they take off again. During the long walk they will be challenged by two more sets of sentries, each set, incidentally, in the uniforms of different branches of the service. Now they arrive at the massive steel door with its blinking light and beep SOUND. Dr. Short flicks a switch to the left of door, speaks into a microphone then steps back. Smoothly, the door slides open, the three men are admitted and the door glides back again.

INT. ROOM

This room, spotless and almost clinical in its bareness, is soon to be delivery room for a momentous birth. Here stands Cerebrac, the most complicated electronic computer ever devised. Millions of indexed histories of adult Americans have gestated for over two years in the iron whom of this infallible thinking machines, only one to be selected as the completely normal American adult. The flashing signal and the BEEP are the signs that delivery is imminent. Combines with the beep now is another SOUND. This is a rhythmic clicking and whirring SOUND rather like steady typing.

CLOSE SHOT—CEREBRAC

It is all you expect it to be. But soon the eye is caught by a glass opening about six inches square. It is an indicator that registers the time in one second intervals and a sign beneath it says:

> COUNTDOWN

There are less than two minutes left to zero.

GROUP SHOT- THE THREE MEN

As they stand to one side, waiting. Only Dr. Short seems a little nervous. Newkirk is quite calm, and John Dolan is looking off at the machine with something rather akin to hostility.

> SHORT
> Less than two minutes.

> NEWKIRK
> Fantastic A machine that is scrutinizing
> the foibles and probing the peccadillo's of
> a hundred million people.

DOLAN
(drily)
A gigantic Peeping Tom.

SHORT
(devoid of humor)
Cerebrac has every virtue but none of the vices of the human, Dr. Dolan.

DOLAN
Sorry, Dr. Short. I had no idea you were so touchy about your iron prodigy.

SHORT
Not touchy. I've waited to years for this moment. In less than two minutes my electronic computer will have selected the one perfectly normal American adult.

NEWKIRK
Too bad Cerebrac can't do the rest of the job, eh John?

DOLAN
On the contrary, I'm looking forward to it.

SHORT
Provide the subject is willing.

DOLAN
(astonished)
Willing? Are you serious? How could he not be willing?

NEWKIRK
(mildly)
Not everybody wants to be the first human to be sent to the moon.

SHORT
Not even the most normal American adult.

DOLAN
Ridiculous. Only an abnormal person would resist. And according to you, Dr. Short, your device is infallible.

The whirring SOUND suddenly becomes erratic. The three heads swing around to the computer. The expressions are tense.

DOLAN
(continuing)
What happened?

NEWKIRK
Could something go wrong?

SHORT
Impossible. It's — it's merely changing rhythm prior to zero.

CLOSE SHOT—GLASS WINDOW ON CEREBRAC

The seconds are ticking off visibly and stand at thirteen as we reach it. The erratic SOUND persists and the CAMERA TRAVELS BEHIND AND DOWN the maze of intricate wiring and tubes. In a tiny aperture near the base of the computer a mouse appears. For a fraction of a second it looks this way and that, then darts back inside Cerebrac. Perhaps we've discovered the reason for the electronic brain's odd behavior.

CLOSE SHOT—GROUP

As they continue to stare. The erratic whirring SOUND continues over the scene, becoming more erratic if anything. INTERCUT with the machine as it approaches zero. The men watch, fascinated, and at last there is a single, bell-like SOUND.

All other SOUNDS CEASE. For a tense, silent moment nobody moves.

Then Dr. Short starts towards the machine, CAMERA FOLLOWING. He goes to a special slot in the machine, reaches in, and pulls out a card.

ANOTHER ANGLE

As Dr. Short rejoins his colleagues. In his hand he holds the large index card. He seems puzzled.

                  DOLAN
Well, what's his name, doctor?

                  SHORT
It's woman.

                  NEWKIRK
A woman?

                  SHORT
                  (firmly)
A woman. The one normal American adult is a woman!...

                  SHORT
                  (Coldly)
I am not entertained by your crass witticism, Dr. Dolan. Why shouldn't it be a woman?

                  NEWKIRK
He's right, John. Why shouldn't it?

                  DOLLAN
Because you can't condition a woman for a flight to the moon. You can't even teach them to throw a baseball.

                  SHORT
The understanding was that you abide by the selection of Cerebrac.

DOLAN
But I have to live with the subject all during the training period!

NEWKIRK
That may be difficult to explain to your fiancée.

DOLAN
Being a woman she won't understand, but I'll explain anyway. What's this something's name?

SHORT
(READING CARD)
She's a dental Technician. Her name is Joan Jones and she lives in Hot Springs, Arkansas.

NEWKIRK
Not really! Isn't that significant? A woman chosen by destiny to save the world.

DOLAN
Stop being cryptic. What's significant?

NEWKIRK
Joan of Arkansas.

DOLAN
Not only a bad pun, but scientifically of little value.

NEWKIRK
Don't you see how fittings it is that she should be trusted to your care, John?

DOLAN
No.

                    NEWKIRK
Joan of Arc gave her life for peace, and the
man who was captured and executed with
here-her constant squire during the bitter
years — you remember his name?

                    DOLAN
Certainly. It was Jean d'Aulon.

                    NEWKIRK
                    (smiling)
You have a good memory, John Dolan.

The parallel strikes, even Short is startled by the analogy, and as he stares at the index card in his hand we ZOOM in to it.

KIND INSERT — INDEX CARD

A complicated SERIES OF HOLES and typewritten information. Featured in the upper left hand corner of the card is an excellent photograph of Joan Jones. She looks trim and attractive in her nurse's cap. As we MOVE IN CLOSER on the photo, seemingly coming from the misty past, softly first, then growing in volume can be HEARD the stirring strains of the Marseillaise.

                                                        FADE OUT

FADE IN:

EXT. HOT SPRINGS, ARKANSAS — DAY — FULL SHOT (STOCK)

                                                        DISSOLVE TO:

EXT. MEDICAL BUILDING — DAY — FULL SHOT (STOCK)

                                                        DISSOLVE TO:

INT. DR. FERGUSON'S DENTAL OFFICES

This is a small dental suite consisting of a reception room, two operating rooms and a tiny lab. Looking down from the lab bench we see a length of hall and the reception room beyond. Midway between the lab and reception room, on the right side of the hall are

the two operating rooms separated by the thickness of one wall. A
FULL SHORT discloses all but the two operating rooms. In the f.g. is
the lab bench, cluttered with the usual dental equipment, a bunsen
burner and small crucible, some models of uppers and lowers,
casts, etc. Gracing the bench, and busily engaged in some difficult
technical maneuvers with inlays and the crucible, is an attractive,
remarkably efficient nurse. This is JOAN JONES. As the melts some
gold, works with tweezers, shapes a cast, she still finds time to crack
an occasional walnut between the modeled teeth. She nibbles while
she works. In the b.g. we see the door open, a light warning bell
SOUNDS, and Dolan enters with Newkirk.

>   JOAN
>   (over her shoulder)
>   One moment, please.

MED, SHOT — DOLAN AND NEWKIRK

At door. They look toward the lab.

> NEWKIRK
> There's your Joan. I must say, Dolan, even
> from this angle she does something for
> that nurse's uniform.

> DOLAN
> (eyeing her critically)
> Gynandroid mesopene combining fart's
> torso with Tittlebat's posture. Probably
> flighty.

> NEWKIRK
> John, she's a woman. Stop thinking of her
> as an index card.

> DOLAN
> She's American's most normal adult,
> selected by Cerebrac to fly to the moon,
> and her training begins this very minute.

>   Go, Newkirk, you have things to do. I'll
>   remain and prepare her.

Newkirk shrugs and exits.

REVERSE ANGLE

As Joan finishes her task. She has softened some wax for an impression and carries it between a pair of forceps. She turns and starts towards the first operating room, CAMERA TRUCKING with her.

INT. OPERATING ROOM

This is regular tiny room containing Ritter sink and drill unit, cabinet and sterilizer. A patient, bibbed, sits in the dental chair facing a window. Joan goes to him, places the wax on a tray on the table unit, squirts water in the patient's mouth.

>   JOAN
>   Rinse and spit.

The patient complies as Joan softens the wax a little more over the small gas flame. Now she opens the man's mouth, positions the wax over the molars, adjusting it with her forefinger.

>   JOAN
>   Bite.

He does so and she barely gets her finger out in time.

>   JOAN
>   (continuing, shaking her head)
>   Mr. Keppler, you certainly snap at a piece
>   of wax! Haven't you had breakfast?
>   (as he starts to talk)
>   Don't talk. Let that set so I can get a good
>   impression for Dr. Ferguson. I'll be right back.

She goes to the reception room, CAMERA FOLLOWING. Dr. Dolan, now seated, is reading a magazine. He rises as she enters.

               DOLAN
Good morning. You're Miss Jones?

               JOAN
Yes. You've never been here before, have
you? Somebody recommend you?

               DOLAN
Do you have recurrent nightmares?

               JOAN
Dr. Ferguson always likes to know when a
new patient is recommend — nightmares?

               DOLAN
Yes.

               JOAN
Well, it might be caused by your teeth — if
you'll just follow me I'll make some X-rays.
           (takes his arm)
Dr. Ferguson insists on a complete set of X-
rays before he does any work on a patient.

She has led him into operating room number two. She eases him into the chair and is already putting a bib around his neck.

               DOLAN
Miss Jones, I did not come here to get my
teeth X-rayed.

               JOAN
       (squirting water in his mouth)
No charge. Here, rinse and spit.

He does so automatically. As he opens his mouth to talk again she already has an X-ray film in his cheek, takes his hand and guides a finger to his mouth.

                        JOAN
                     (continuing)
         Hold that right there.

He does so and she aims the bullet-shaped X-ray machine at the proper spot, presses the button, removes the film, reaches for another.

                        DOLAN
         Miss Jones, you're just wasting that film.

                        JOAN
                  (shoving it in his mouth)
         That's what you think. Hold that...
                     (aims the X-ray)
         You should see what turns up on some of
         these pictures.
                     (presses the button)
         Especially if you don't aim exactly right.

She takes the film out, starts to get another.

                        DOLAN
                     (stares at her)
         Are you quite finished?

                        JOAN
         Never saw it to fall. The bigger the man
         the more scared he is about — oops — I
         forgot Mr. Keppler. Sit Still.

She flies out of the room, CAMERA FOLLOWING, and into the other one.

                        JOAN
                  (grabbing tweezers)
         There we are. Open up please.

Mr. Keppler tries to open his mouth, but no dice.

                        JOAN
         Oh, dear. I let it set too long.

She gets behind him and tries to pull his jaws open. They won't come apart, so she tries a lever action with a flat instrument.

INT. OTHER OPERATING ROOM—FULL SHOT

Dolan, hearing the commotion in the other room, gets out of the chair and exits, CAMERA FOLLOWING.

He enter the room where Joan is trying vainly to pry the ma's mouth open.

                        JOAN
                     (top Dolan)
         Here, you try. The wax must have set
         awful — ohhhhh!

Something has suddenly struck her.

                        DOLAN
         What is it?

                        JOAN
         I'll be right back.

She charges out of the room towards the lab. Dolan experimentally tries to get Mr. Kepler's mouth open. Joan returns, white faced.

                        JOAN
         We'd better get Dr. Ferguson.

                        DOLAN
         I'm a doctor. What is it?

                        JOAN
         I'm not sure. Instead of using wax I think
         I used cement.

She grabs a small chisel and dentist's hammer. Dolan restrains her.

                    DOLAN
          Here, here. We'll find out what you used.

He lifts the syringe from the unit, forcing the tip into the corner of Keppler's mouth, squirts in some warm water. Joan, in the meantime, is back of the patient, trying to pull his jaws open.

                    JOAN
          Is the water hot enough?

Mr. Keppler's grimace shows that it is. Suddenly his jaws fly open. Joan, all hysteria gone now, suddenly becomes the efficient nurse again. She removes the impression, and squirts water in Keppler's mouth.

                    JOAN
          Rinse and spit.
                    (to Dolan)
          Now, if you'll go back to your chair, I'll
          finish the x-rays.
                    (to Keppler)
          You sit still while I heat up a fresh bunch
          of wax for the other molars.

Joan starts for the lab, followed by Dolan. As soon as she leaves the room Keppler leaps up from the chair and runs out of the suite still bibbed. We have the feeling he'll never come back.

INT. LAB—FULL SHOT

As Joan works at the bench. She's not conscious that Dolan is standing behind her, and he reacts violently as she cracks a walnut in the false set of teeth. Keppler's leaving has caused the warning BELL to ring, and Joan, assuming a new patient has entered, calls over her shoulder.

                    JOAN
          One moment, please.

                    DOLAN
Miss Jones —

Joan is rather surprised to see him. She lifts the mass of softened wax with the forceps, starts to go.

                    DOLAN
                (blocking her)
        I'm Dr. Dolan and I've come to take you
        back with me to Washington, D.C.

He flashed some kind of identification.

                    JOAN
        Really? Well, I've never been to
        Washington and I'm sure it's a lovely
        place, but I'm not going there with you or
        anyone else — did that say Secret Service?

                    DOLAN
        More important and more secret.

                    JOAN
                (backing up a little)
        I haven't done anything wrong — I pay my taxes —

                    DOLAN
        Miss Jones — you've been chosen.

                    JOAN
                (a little frightened)
        Well, that's too bad — let them choose
        somebody else. Please, I've got a patient in
        the other room.

                    DOLAN
        Your patient left. Put your things on,
        you're coming with me.

JOAN
(fighting for time)
But I can't leave on such short notice — I have to get my bags packed and — and —

Newkirk enters carrying two valises.

DOLAN
Your bags are packed. Professor Newkirk attended to it.

Newkirk enters the tiny lab and sets the suitcases down. It's getting a little crowded and Joan is getting panicky.

JOAN
What is this? Where'd you get my bags?

NEWKIRK
At your house, Miss Jones. Your fatherhelped pack them.

DOLAN
We have no time to waste.

JOAN
(wildly)
Wait. I can't just pick up and leave like this — give me a couple of weeks — after all I have to give Dr. Ferguson notice — he can't get along without me —

The door opens and DR. FERGUSON enters. He goes right to the lab —

JOAN
(as she sees him)
Isn't that right, Dr. Ferguson — you can't spare me now. They want me to go to Washington with —

                    FERGUSON
I know, Joan —

                     JOAN
                   (to Dolan)
You see! He can't spare me. It takes time
to get somebody who is qualified to…

A stunning young lady in a nurse's uniform enters, comes into lab.

                    PERGUSON
                 (introducing her)
This is my new nurse, Miss Kelly.

The little lab is now terribly crowded. Joan looks from one to the other like a trapped animal.

                     DOLAN
                   (peremptory)
Ready, Miss Jones?

                    FERGUSON
                 (a little abashed)
I'm sorry — I wasn't allowed to prepare
you, Joan — you'll find out why later.

                     JOAN
Uh-huh.

                    FERGUSON
I'll be seeing your family — do you have
any message for them? Is there any word
you'd like to leave?

                     JOAN
Yes. Just one word.

                    FERGUSON
What is it?

                    JOAN
        Help.

As Dolan and Newkirk escort her out,

                                    DISSOLVE TO:

22 EXT. SPEEDING TRAIN—NIGHT—FULL SHOT (STOCK)

                                DISSOLVE THROUGH:

23 INT. TRAIN COMPARTMENT—MED. SHOT

Joan, now dressed in a traveling outfit. Is seated, staring out the window. There is a KNOCK AT THE DOOR.

                    JOAN
              (without turning)
        Come in!

Newkirk enters.

                  NEWKIRK
        Everything all right, Miss Jones?

                    JOAN
        Of course. Why not?

                  NEWKIRK
        Well, I thought you might be a little bit
        disturbed over…

                    JOAN
        Disturbed? After all, what happened?
        I was just Shanghaied, done out of my
        job, had my life ruined without knowing
        why… what could be wrong?

                  NEWKIRK
        Uh…

JOAN
Let me put it this way... what more could
be wrong?

NEWKIRK
I am sorry, I can't tell you.

JOAN
Why?

NEWKIRK
I am sorry, I can't tell you.

JOAN
Then who can?

Dolan enters.

DOLAN
I can, Miss Jones. Stand up, please.

JOAN
What?

DOLAN
Newkirk... the girl has a hearing
impairment!

NEWKIRK
No, no, perfectly normal.

He encourages Joan to stand, which she does. Dolan surveys her from all sides. He finally shrugs.

DOLAN
Oh, well.

JOAN
That's a nasty thing to say!

                    DOLAN
You may sit down.

Not knowing what else to do, she sits.

                    DOLAN
Miss Jones. It has taken a great deal of time, millions of dollars, and the best brains in the country to find you.

                    JOAN
                  (helpfully)
I'm in the phone book.

                    DOLAN
You were in the phone book. Operation Selection being over, operation Conditioning begins. You are now Subject X.

                    JOAN
Me?

                    DOLAN
There will be sacrifices, of course… which will have to be made by both of us.

                    JOAN
                  (on guard)
Like what?

                    DOLAN
You will be subjected to mental and physical exhaustion, sleeplessness, extremes of hot and cold, close confinement in cramped quarters, and long periods without food.

> JOAN
> What sacrifices are you making?

> DOLAN
> I was to have been married to- night, but that will have to wait. I think that explains everything... any loose ends?

> JOAN
> Just one. What's this all about?

Dolan surveys here, but speaks to Newkirk.

> DOLAN
> Remarkable how persistent she is... slight touch of monomania?

> NEWKIRK
> You really haven't told her, John.

> DOLAN
> Oh.
> (to Joan)
> I delayed...

There is a KNOCK AT THE DOOR.

> DOLAN
> (continuing)
> Come in!

A waiter enters, with a heavily laden tray.

> DOLAN
> (continuing)
> I ordered supper here.
> (to waiter)
> Just set it up, please.

The waiter puts down the tray, and starts setting a table.

> DOLAN
> (continuing, resuming)
> I delayed telling you any details, until
> now, Miss Jones, because while, our
> mission is essentially just a matter of
> scientific routine...

He casually checks the food as he talks, lifting some of the hot covers.

> JOAN
> (slightly relieved)
> Just routine.

> DOLAN
> Yes. I wanted to avoid an initial reaction
> of typically feminine hysteria.

Joan, slightly nettled, matches his action of checking the food. She is being casual.

> JOAN
> I think that I'm fairly well composed,
> Doctor... fire away.

> DOLAN
> (very causal)
> You, Miss Jones, are to be the first human
> being to make a flight to the moon.

> JOAN
> Make a flight to the moon.

> DOLAN
> Yes.

Joan casually raises a cover, sniffs the food, puts down the cover and then suddenly leaps up, tries to get one foot out of the window.

> JOAN
> Stop the train! I'm getting off!

She yanks the emergency cord, and there is a SHRIEK OF BRAKES. The compartment lurches violently, and Joan, Dolan, Newkirk, the waiter, and the food all go to the floor, in a violent tangle. Dolan removes a bit of club sandwich from his hair, and speaks acidly to Newkirk.

> DOLAN
> There you are, Newkirk. If she's this
> hysterical on a train how will she be have
> in a rocket?

Woman-like, Joan bursts into tears.

DISSOLVE TO:

24. ESTABLISHING SHOTS—WASHINGTON—NIGHT (STOCK)

DISSOLVE TO:

25. INT. LIVING ROOM—FULL SHOT

The room is furnished in good taste, but tending toward severity, reflecting the personality of Dolan, who is entering with Joan and Newkirk. They put down their luggage.

> DOLAN
> (calling)
> Mrs. Putnam! Mrs. Putnam!
> (to Joan)
> I trust this will be satisfactory, Miss Jones?

> JOAN
> (looking around)
> It's not bad. Of course, I'll give it a few
> feminine touches.

> DOLAN
> They are all the same, Newkirk. Down through the ages they have massacred architecture, sabotaged home furnishing, and have smothered the art of the decorator in amass of ruffles... all in the name of the feminine touch.
> (to Joan)
> Do not alter the position of a single ash tray!
> (turning)
> Ah, Mrs. Putnam. Where were you?

MRS. PUTNAM has entered, being apparently roused out of bed.

> PUTNAM
> I was asleep.

> DOLAN
> At one in the morning?

> NEWKIRK
> Mrs. Putnam, this is Miss Jones. You take good care of her.

> JOAN
> How do you do, Mrs. Putnam?

> PUTNAM
> Nice to know you, Miss Jones. I'll get you unpacked, and...

> PUTNAM
> Nice to know you, Miss Jones. I'll get you unpacked, and...
> (in the act of picking up Joan's bags, she stops; to Dolan:)
> Miss Jones?

DOLAN
Of course.

PUTNAM
But you told me she was to be a man!

DOLAN
(impatiently)
Really, Mrs. Putnam... what's the difference?

JOAN
(to Newkirk)
Is he serious?

DOLAN
Just get her unpacked, Mrs. Putnam.

PUTNAM
Yes, Dr. Dolan.

She exits, with Joan's bags, to an adjoining bedroom.

DOLAN
(turning to Joan)
Well.

JOAN
(a bit uncertain)
Well... goodnight.

DOLAN
Where are you going?

JOAN
Me? I thought you were going.

DOLAN
Where would I go?... I live here.

JOAN
(backing up)
Oh, no you don't!

DOLAN
Newkirk! I refuse to put up with this!

NEWKIRK
(placating Joan)
Dolan and I both have quarters here, Miss Jones. And his laboratory is here.

JOAN
(somewhat mollified)
Oh.

NEWKIRK
And Mrs. Putnam is here, of course.

JOAN
Well...

DOLAN
So stop all this nonsense and get your clothes off.

JOAN
I'd rather die!

DOLAN
(disgusted again)
In your room, naturally. And put on a hospital gown. I have to give you a complete physical examination.

>   (as she stares)
>   I am a doctor!
>
>   NEWKIRK
>   (intervening)
>   Dr. Dolan... it's one o'clock... couldn't this
>   wait till morning?
>
>   DOLAN
>   It is morning! However, there's one thing I
>   must do tonight. This way.

He motions for Joan to follow, and goes to a door, CAMERA MOVING WITH THEM.

MED. CLOSE SHOT—AT DOOR

Dolan opens the door, and motions Joan through.

>   DOLAN
>   In there, please... I'll be right in.

He closes the door after she exits. From a cabinet he takes out and puts on a lead apron, long lead gloves, and finally a lead helmet which goes over his head. He then goes through the door.

INT. LAB—FULL SHOT

As Dolan enters. Joan stares. Dolan takes up a long pole with an alligator claw on the end of it, and with the claw maneuvers open a wall safe, with a thick door. He reaches in with the claw, extracts a lead cup, and hands sit to Joan on the end of the pole.

>   DOLAN
>   Drink this.
>
>   JOAN
>   (horrified)
>   Drink it yourself, you—monster!

She runs out of the lab.

INT. LIVING ROOM—FULL SHOT

As Newkirk watches, Joan runs across the living room, tries to get a foot out the window, fails, and runs to the door of her bedroom.

MED. SHOT—AT DOOR

Mrs. Putnam comes out of the door as Joan rushes up to it. She stares as Joan goes in, and slams the door. Mrs. Putnam turns, then represses a small shriek.

POV SHOT—DOLAN

He is walking into the living room, still holding the cup with the tongs.

FULL SHOT—MLIVING ROOM

Dolan puts down the cup and takes off the helmet. Mrs. Putnam crosses, giving him a look, and exits.

      NEWKIRK
 What happened?

      DOLAN
 She's totally unreasonable, Newkirk!
 Where did she go?

      NEWKIRK
 Her room.

      DOLAN
 Crying, I suppose.

      NEWKIRK
 Or packing.

      DOLAN
 Well, let her pack! I won't stop here!

She's totally devoid of any semblance of rationality!

NEWKIRK
While you are the epitome of reason.

DOLAN
Of course I am. Are you siding with her?

Newkirk speaks with a humor which Dolan totally misses.

NEWKIRK
I can hardly help myself.

DOLAN
Why?

NEWKIRK
You're forgetting your history. Every soldier in the French army was in love with Joan of arc.

DOLAN
But that's utterly...
(breaks off)
At your age?

NEWKIRK
At my age I no longer have to worry. But you...

DOLAN
(sputtering)
Me? Has everyone gone mad? Why, I... she... that's the most...

Newkirk motions him to silence, as he sees Joan's door opening. Both look.

POV SHOT—JOAN

She comes out of her room, wearing a dressing gown. She has calmed down.

> JOAN
> What you wanted me to drink... was it important?

FULL SHOT—LIVING ROOM

> DOLAN
> Of course it's important! Radioactive isotopes.

> JOAN
> But you wouldn't go near it!

> NEWKIRK
> Dr. Dolan just wears the protective equipment because of the cumulative effect of radiation. He's done it many times.

> JOAN
> (suspicious again)
> How many have you lost before me?

> DOLAN
> They were all monkeys, and delightful to work with! Now drink it!

> JOAN
> (drinks it)
> Needs a twist of lemon.

> NEWKIRK
> Good girl.

                    JOAN
Now can I go to bed?

                    DOLAN
Of course. Just slip this on, while you sleep.

From a nearby cabinet, he extracts an encephalograph head band, which he puts on Joan's head. A long wire trails.

                    JOAN
What is it?

                    DOLAN
Encephalograph. It's important we chart your brain waves.

                    JOAN
Brain waves. Well... good night.

Wires trailing, she starts to her room.

                    NEWKIRK
Goodnight.

                    JOAN
                (turning back)
That stuff I drank... what was it for?

                    DOLAN
We use it in measuring the effect of cosmic radiation.

                    JOAN
Cosmic radiation?

                    DOLAN
Yes. Tomorrow we shoot you into the ionosphere.

Joan stares at him, then takes off the apparatus and jams it down over his head.

                    JOAN
          Chart your own brain waves... You're
          gone! Gone!

She marches into her room and slams the door. Dolan, his dignity badly ruffled, glares after her.

                    DOLAN
          The woman's impossible, Newkirk!
          Completely impossible!

                                                    FADE OUT

                    END OF ACT ONE

                        ACT TWO

FADE IN:

INT. GROUND CONTROL—CLOSE SHOT—SCHEMATIC DRAWING

This is a cross section of an advanced type of jet aircraft. Fitted for space travel. It contains three seats one behind the other, portholes above the seats and a fair sized instrument panel up front. In front of the pilot's seat is a steering device, and several levers rise from the floor in the f.g. and line the wall in the rear. CAMERA PULLS BACK to disclose the drawing is on a blackboard in the Control Room. Standing at the drawing, pointer in hand, is Henry Newkirk.

                    NEWKIRK
          You understand, Garrison, ground control
          will take over at five thousand feet and
          remain in control until landing.

CAMERA PULLS BACK Still further and we see he is addressing a pilot. He nods.

WIDER ANGLE

To reveal the entire interior of the Control Room. Dolan enters. He looks haggard, as though he spent a sleepless night, In one hand he clutches a long piece of graph paper with erratic tracings on it. Exhausted, he flips into a chair. Newkirk looks at him with concern.

      NEWKIRK
Well, how did it go last night, John?

      DOLAN
Miserable. I never closed my eyes for a minute.

      NEWKIRK
Miss Jones?

      DOLAN
Miss Jones. I had the ball is to graph attached to her bad. Newkirk, that woman is a mouth breather and is suffering from Kleinfeld's Stertor.

      NEWKIRK
Pardon?

      DOLAN
She snores!
      (shakes chart)
And I didn't need this ballistograph to tell me, either! My eardrums are shattered! She not only snores, She whines, gurgles and snarls, and to think I have to suffer thru this for the next five years —

NEWKIRK
(interrupting)
John. John! Miss Jones was not snoring — I was.

DOLAN
(stunned)
Newkirk!

NEWKIRK
John, I changed rooms with her. She said she wanted to get as far away from you as possible.

DOLAN
I won't have it! Newkirk, are you a scientific investigator or a puling participant in an adolescent slumber party?

Dr. short enters during Dolan's last speech.

SHORT
Dr. Dolan, I demand you cancel the ionospheric flight experiment! The subject cannot possibly be prepared and all you'll do is make Cerebrac look bad.

DOLAN
Cerebrac couldn't look any worse than it does now. A lottery drum could have made a better selection!

NEWKIRK
John, you're not being fair.

DOLAN
Why do you constantly defend this unstable woman?

                    SHORT
You're asking this poor girl, without an
ounce of previous experience, to submit
to a series of shock tests that would try
the courage of a lion tamer!

                    DOLAN
If she's normal, she'll survive. If she isn't,
it's best to find out now.
                    (to pilot)
Get the pressure suits ready. Check all the
instruments and communications and be
prepared to take off in thirty minutes.

He exits.

                                        DISSOLVE TO

INT. AIRCRAFT—FULL SHOT

This is the aircraft seen earlier in the schematic drawing. Joan, in a pressure suit and helmet is seated in the center seat. The pilot and Dolan are also in pressure suits. Joan peeps out of the porthole alongside. She reacts, then whirls on Dolan.

                    JOAN
You lied to me! You said you were flying
meback to hot Springs! You lied to me.

                    DOLAN
                    (calmly)
I said we'd be flying over Hot Springs.

                    JOAN
We're nowhere near it.
                    (pointing down)
You can't fool me! We're over New York.
I can see Central Park Lake and the
rowboats.

DOLAN
That's the Atlantic Ocean and the Seventh Fleet.

JOAN
Atlan — how high are we?

DOLAN
Not more than thirty miles.

JOAN
Thirty miles!

She leaps up and tries to get a foot out of the window. Dolan restrains her, pushes her back in her seat. The cabin angles up as though climbing.

DOLAN
Never jump out during a climb.

JOAN
(hysterical)
I wanna get out of here. I can't stand high altitudes. I get nose-bleeds when I sleep in an upper berth!

DOLAN
Sit still. I'm trying to record your vascular reaction to the increasing pressure and I can't make any findings if you persist in jumping about like a frog on a griddle!

JOAN
Well, make him land this buck Rogers special and let me out.

DOLAN
Not until I've recorded the apex of your diastole.

                        JOAN
          Oh no! I've had enough of this!

Starts to go for the window again, he pushed her back. Dolan fastens her seat belt.

CLOSE SHOT—DOLAN

Reseating himself he talks in a low voice into a tiny mike in his lapel.

                        DOLAN
              Ground control. Dolan.

                                                CUT TO:

INT. GROUND CONTROL—CLOSE SHOT—SHORT AND NEWKIRK

They are seated before a radar screen and guidance system. Dolan's voice comes over scene.

                   DOLAN'S VOICE (o.s.)
              Subject is threatening to jump... I shall
              now proceed according to plan...

                                                CUT TO:

INT. AIRCRAFT—CLOSE SHOT—JOAN

                        JOAN
                (tapping pilot on shoulder)
              Listen, You! You land this thing or I'll kick
              a hole in the window and jump out!

FULL SHOT INT.

                        DOLAN
              Miss Jones, if you wish to leave, all you
              have to do is pull the lever alongside of
              you. The one marked "EJECT".

JOAN
(looking around wildly)
Where?
(she sees it)
You think I'm afraid, huh?

DOLAN
Quite frankly, yes.

JOAN
You sound pretty anxious to get rid of me.

DOLAN
(innocently)
I? On the contrary, Miss Jones, I find you company more than stimulating.
(barks)
But if you are going to stay, sit still and be quiet!

JOAN
(grabbing the lever)
That does it! You can't yell at me! I'm leaving!

She sets her jaw, shuts her eyes and yanks on the lever. Nothing happens to her, but THE PILOT IS EJECTED with a mighty SHOOSH!

JOAN
(eyes still closed)
Well, this isn't so bad.
(she opens her eyes cautiously, one at a time)
Well!

She suddenly sees that the pilot and his seat are gone.

JOAN
What happened? I must have pulled the wrong one!

                    DOLAN
It would appear so.

                    JOAN
                 (panicky)
But we're thirty miles up and no pilot! Do
something—take the controls!

                    DOLAN
I haven't the vaguest idea how to fly this
thing.

                    JOAN
              (getting her belt open)
How can you be so calm?
       (she gets out of her seat, goes to control
            panel in the pitching cabin)
There must be some way to get this
thingdown.

She tries several knobs, levers and wheels. The cabin lurches and rolls violently, Joan stumbling and falling with every new spin. If Dolan were not secured to his seat he would go flying. He talks into his little mike.

CLOSE SHOT—DOLAN

As he talks to ground control.

                    DOLAN
Reaction normal. She's in a panic. She
thinks she's flying the plane.

                                           CUT TO:

INT. GROUND CONTROL—SHORT AND NEWKIRK

Apparently some trouble has developed because both men are working feverishly at the control equipment.

>   NEWKIRK
>   (into mike)
>   John! She is flying the plane! We've lost
>   ground control!

                                                    CUT TO:

INT. AIRCRAFT

Dolan reacts violently. Joan struggles with the lurching ship.

                                                    CUT TO:

INT. GROUND CONTROL—NEWKIRK AND SHORT

At the radar screen. The blip is going thru an amazing series of acrobatics. At one time it seems to divide into two separate blips, then it blends into one again. Short is working frantically with the knobs and dials on the guidance system.

>   DOLAN'S VOICE
>   If I can get this wild woman back in her
>   seat I'll eject her and abandon ship.

                                                    CUT TO:

INT. AIRCRAFT

As Dolan tries to unbuckle his safety belt and get to Joan she pulls on some Dolan goes hurtling out of the cabin and thru the roof. Joan picks herself up, looks around and sees nobody. She looks up at the opening in the roof.

>   JOAN
>   (yelling up)
>   Go off and leave me—you big coward!

She get into her seat, buckles the belt, and bracing herself, eyes closed, she pulls another "EJECT" LEVER. The ship goes into an almost vertical climb, but nothing else happens. She opens her eyes.

                                                    CUT TO:

INT. GOURND CONTROL—NEWKIRK AND SHORT

Short working, Newkirk at the radar screen. The blip is climbing straight up.

> NEWKIRK
> Good heavens! She's going into an anti-gravity orbit!

The blip has climbed into an ascending parabola.

> SHORT
> I've got this in order again, but they'll have to come out of that orbit before it's of any use. Give Dolan instructions.

> NEWKIRK
> (into mike)
> John. Can you hear me?

CUT TO:

INT. AIRCRAFT

Joan can't understand why she's still there. She fumbles with another lever.

> NEWKIRK'S VOICE
> John. Can you here me?

Suddenly Joan's helmet floats lazily up towards the roof of the cabin. Absently Joan reaches for it, puts it on again, and goes for the lever again. Once more the helmet floats upwards and she repeats the operation. The third time it gets away from her, remains glued to the roof of the cabin. Joan unbuckles her safety belt in order to retrieve the helmet and now completely weightless, she floats in gentle maneuvers until she, too, reaches the cabin roof. (TRAVELLING MAT) Her efforts to regain gravity result in a ludicrous twisting and turning but she can't get down other objects, loosened in flight, now begin to float up to her and she fights them off like attacker's bullets.

CUT TO:

INT. GOURND CONTROL- NEWKIRK AND SHORT

NEWKIRK
(at radar screen)
Short! Look here!
(he points to a smaller blip on screen)
No wonder Dolan doesn't answer — he ejected himself.

SHORT
He showed the white feather and left that poor girl up there by herself.

NEWKIRK
We've got to talk her down.
(into mike)
Miss Jones. Miss Jones — is Professor Newkirk. Can you hear me?

CUT TO:

INT AIRCRAFT

Joan is still pinned to the ceiling. She squirms around as his voice is HEARD.

JOAN
I can hear you fine! Where are you?

CUT TO:

INT. GROUND CONTROL — NEWKIRK AND SHORT

NEWKIRK
Miss Jones — if I am getting thru — listen carefully... you'll be out of the anti-gravity orbit in exactly nine seconds... As soon as you feel weight returning walk down

the side of the cabin... Buckle yourself in
your seat and we will bring you to a safe
landing.

CUT TO:

INT. AIRCRAFT

Joan, still on the ceiling, hears the last part of Newkirk's instructions. She makes a tentative try at walking down the side wall, and much to her amazement she succeeds. Gravity returned, she flies to her seat and buckles herself in.

                NEWKIRK'S VOICE
      Now, Miss Jones, it's imperative that you
      brace yourself against dive shock—

Joan braces herself by grabbing the two "EJECT" levers on either side of her seat. As the plane tilts forward she naturally presses the levers forward. In a trice she is ejected out of the ship at lightning speed.

                NEWKIRK'S VOICE
         (continuing, to the empty plane)
      —being particularly careful not to touch
      the two eject levers alongside your seat.
      Now—

FADE OUT

FADE IN:

INT. DOLAN LIVING ROOM—NIGHT—FULL SHOT

Newkirk is seated, smoking and reading a scientific journal. He looks up as Mrs. Putnam comes out of Joan's room, and gives her an inquiring glance. She meets his glance by shaking her head, and goes on across the room. The front door opens quickly and Dolan rushes in. he strips off his hat and coat, exposing the fact that he has a narrow bandage around his head. Coming into the room, he hands his hat and coat to Mrs. Putnam.

                    DOLAN
    Thanks, Mrs. Putnam.
            (refers to bandage)
    Don't worry about this. Fortunately, I
    landed in a cherry tree.

                    PUTNAM
    That's too bad.

She exits. Dolan stares after her for a moment, but doesn't sense the chill in the room. He goes to Newkirk.

                    DOLAN
    Couldn't get away from those
    incompetents at the hospital, Newkirk.
    They insisted on... Where's Joan?

                    NEWKIRK
    Joan?

                    DOLAN
            (impatiently)
    Miss Jones, Miss Jones! I want to get busy
    on my follow-up tests to the flight.

                    NEWKIRK
    She's in her room.

                    DOLAN
    Good.

He starts forward.

                    NEWKIRK
    Packing.

                    DOLAN
    This is no time for a holiday!

NEWKIRK
She's going back to Arkansas.

DOLAN
Whatever for?

NEWKIRK
(after looking at him)
Just unreasonable.

DOLAN
She is unreasonable, of course, but
that's only because she's a woman.
But I've developed something in her,
Newkirk... courage! And by the time I
give her five years more of conditioning...

Joan has come out of her room on the last of this speech, carrying her bags.

JOAN
I won't be with you for five more years,
Dr. Dolan. Or five months, five weeks,
five days, or five seconds. I'm going back
to Arkansas, and you can't stop me!
You... you assassin!

Dolan indicates his bandage.

DOLAN
Don't worry about this... it's just a
scratch.

JOAN
That's too bad.

DOLAN
Thank you. Let me take your bags.

She jerks them back from him.

> JOAN
> You try and stop me and I'll call the police!

> DOLAN
> Stop you? I'll carry your bags to the depot. It's just a few blocks.

> JOAN
> I'm a mature woman, my mind is made up and I know my rights under the constitution: I'm leaving!

> DOLAN
> (looking at his watch)
> I think we can make the mid-night train.

> JOAN
> I warn you, nothing you can do or say will make any difference! I'm leaving!

He picks up her bags.

> DOLAN
> Shall we go?

> JOAN
> (bitterly)
> You take the fun out of everything!

DISSOVE TO:

INT. LONG CORRIDOR—NIGHT -MOVING SHOT

Joan and Dolan are proceeding down the corridor. Dolan carrying Joan's bag. Joan suddenly stops.

JOAN
                (suspiciously)
        I won't go a step further. I know this isn't
        the railroad station.

                    DOLAN
        No, it's not the railroad station.

                    JOAN
        Where are you taking me?

                    DOLAN
        Oh, I'm going to take you to the train all
        right. Right after we make this call.

                    JOAN
        On whom?

                    DOLAN
        You'll see. Come on.

As they move forward again they are challenged by a Secret Service man. Dolan flashes his identification. They are given a salute and they pass through.

                                        DISSOLVE TO:

INT. EXECUTIVE OFFICE—FULL SHOT

CAMERA IS SHOOTING TOWARD Joan, from the other side of the room, over the top of the executive desk. A man's shoulder is visible over the back of the chair, behind the desk. Joan is at the door on the other side of the room, awed.

                    THE CHIEF
                (his voice is sonorous)
        Come in, please.

JOAN
(coming forward)
Yes, sir.

She gazes around in awe, and trips slightly, righting herself against the desk of the CHIEF.

MED. CLOSE SHOT—JOAN

JOAN
Excuse me.

THE CHIEF
Not at all. A chair.

JOAN
No, I think I'd rather stand. I'll feel better.

THE CHIEF
Of course, Miss Jones.

JOAN
You... know my name?

THE CHIEF
Some day. Miss Jones, our whole country will know it.

JOAN
But you don't understand... sir. I'm going back to Hot springs. I'm not suited for this... they made a mistake. Sir

THE CHIEF
Are you sure?

JOAN
Of course I'm sure. I'm a dental

technician, and that's all I want to be, and...
>(breaks off, peering)

You ought to get that fixed, sir. Do you have good dentist?
>(laughs at herself)

I guess you do, huh?

> THE CHIEF
> (slowly)

Joan... of Arkansas. I'd like you to take this, Joan.

CLOSE SHOT—DESK

The chief's arm pushes across an 18-inch statue of Joan of Arc. CAMERA PULLS BACK as Joan take it up, and stares at it.

> JOAN

Joan of Arc.

> THE CHIEF

A young woman... like you not trained for

leadership, fame, the command of an army... but it was a time of great crisis... a time like today.

Joan is almost hypnotized by the voice and the statue.

> JOAN

A time like... today.

> THE CHIEF

And as all Frances suffered, and struggled, and longed for a strong man... a woman came, from the little village of Domremy...

                    JOAN
The little village of... Hot springs.

                 THE CHIEF
Her beauty, her flaming spirit electrified
the defeated and discouraged armies of
France, and Joan, with her faithful squire
Jean d'Aulon by her side...

                    JOAN
Faithful and adoring John Dolan by her
side...

                 THE CHIEF
Rallied the lily banners of France, and led
them to... victoire!

Over the last speech, CAMERA CLOSES IN on Joan, holding the statuette of Joan of Arc. There is a

                         SHIMMERING DISSOLVE:

EXT. FRONT OF STONE ARCH—JOAN—MATCHING SHOT

The SHIMMERING DISSOLVE CLEARS to find Joan in the armor of Joan of Arc, holding a sword in place of the statuette. CAMERA PULLS BACK to reveal Joan in front of a stone arch, surrounded by her followers.

(The Chief's voice has continued, changed from English to French on the word "victoire." Over the following he is describing the scene at Orleans, where the dramatic appearance of Joan of Arc spurred the French troops on to raise the siege and rout the hitherto invincible English.)

Over the voice of The Chief, Joan brandishes her sword.

                    JOAN
Les soldats de France... avant!

She again brandishes her sword.

EXT. BATTLEFIELD SCENE — LONG VIEW — (STOCK)

The French army surges forward to join the issue with the English invader.

MONTAGE — BATTLE SCENES — (STOCK)

Joan, mounted on her charger, is SUPERRED OVER the battle mortage, encouraging her troops and waving her sword. The Chief's voice is heard over this, describing in excited French the battles won by the French, led by Joan.

QUICK DISSOLVE:

THE ARCH — ANOTHER ANGLE

The Chief's voice has changed to sorrow, as he described in French how Joan — betrayed by the Dauphin she had caused to be crowned King, has been captured by the English and is sentenced to be burned at the stake.

Joan is now led in, and tied to the stake which is erected in front of the arch. The faggots are piled around her, and a figure comes forward to light the pyre. He turns TO CAMERA with a wicked grin, and we see it is the face of John Dolan. CAMERA MOVES IN, and the smoke from his torch OBSCURES THE PICTURE.

OIL DISSOLVE:

INT. EXECUTIVE OFFICE — CLOSE SHOT-JOAN

She is standing transfixed, still holding the statuette. The Chief's voice changes back into English.

> THE CHIEF
> ... But Joan had won, for her country was free ... forevermore.

Joan, without a word, does a military turn and marches toward the door. CAMERA MOVES WITH HER.

JOAN
(raising the statuette)
Les soldates de France...avant!

She marches through the open door and out.

INT. CORRIDOR—MED. SHOT

Dolan looks up as Joan marches out. He is in the act of lighting a cigarette, and has just struck a match.

DOLAN
Joan.

She turns and sees him.

JOAN
Pyromaniac!

She slaps the match from his hand and goes off down the corridor, leaving him starting after her. He then looks into the office of The Chief, gets a sign from him, and answer it with an "O.K." sign of his own.

FADE OUT

FADE IN:

INT. DOLAN'S LIVING ROOM—DAY—FULL SHOT

A table is set up in the centre of the room and Mrs. Putnam is serving Joan and Newkirk a hearty breakfast. Joan appears quite relaxed and we gather she is resigned to her new life. Dolan enters, straddles a chair close to Joan, stares at her for a second and the reacts a little uncomfortably. She stops eating.

DOLAN
Eat Hearty. Miss Jones. That'll be the last food you'll have for two weeks.

Joan drops her knife and fork with a clatter.

                    JOAN
What!

                    DOLAN
Miss Jones, the most difficult psychological aspect of aspect travel is complete and utter isolation. Tomorrow at six thirty five a.m. we leave.

                    JOAN
For the moon?

                    DOLAN
Of course not. I am taking you to a small deserted island off the northern coast of Maine.

                    DOLAN
I not only can... I will. There is no water on the island to speak of, only one stagnant pool.

                    JOAN
                 (shrugging)
Well, I don't drink much water anyway.

                    DOLAN
The only food you'll eat is what you'll catch.

                    JOAN
I'm pretty fast on my feet.

                    DOLAN
There's no existing shelter and you'll have great difficulty in keeping warm.

                    JOAN
Oh I'll manage somehow... a deserted
island, huh?

                    DOLAN
Completely deserted.

                    JOAN
For two whole weeks.

                    DOLAN
Precisely.

                    JOAN
                (wistfully)
Just you and me.

                    DOLAN
Just you.

                    JOAN
                (reacting)
Just me... I thought you said you were
taking me!

                    DOLAN
I am. I'll drop you there and pick you up
in two weeks.

Dolan exits without another look at her. Joan stares at Newkirk. He gives her a commiserating shrug, then her provident nature takes over, she picks up her bag off the floor, opens it and scoops all the food from the breakfast dishes into it... as we —

                                                FADE OUT

THE END

SQUEEGEE

Starring Ben Blue

FADE IN:

FULL SHOT—SQUEEGEE'S ROOM—DAY

This is a small attic room which could only be put up for rent by a shameless landlord and only made livable by the ingenuity of the occupant. The ceiling slants down to within several feet of the floor on one side of the room, where Squeegee is asleep in a bed. On the side of the room where the ceiling reaches a respectable height there is an improvised kitchen set-up, with a hotplate. Fans and dishes are arranged in compact fashion along the wall. In the adjoining corner there is a ringed shower-curtain, alongside which is an infant's crib. Everything about the room 'reflects' the character of its occupant, Squeegee... poverty, ingenuity, and neatness.

CAMERA MOVES IN on an alarm clock on a small table to the right of the hot plate. It is seven o'clock. The alarm is due to go off, but the clock has no bell. Instead, we see the clapper moving violently, pulling a string, which is attached to it.

CLOSE SHOT—HOTPLATE

The string from the alarm clock is attached to an old-fashioned burner handle on the gas hotplate. It agitates the handle over so that the gas goes from low to high. A kettle, which has been simmering on the stove, suddenly gives off a loud siren blast as it starts boiling.

CLOSE SHOT—SQUEEGEE

As the kettle sounds off, Squeegee sits bolt upright in bed, banging his head loudly against the low ceiling, and falling back immediately on to the bed.

FULL SHOT—ROOM

As the kettle continues to blast, Squeegee rolls out of the bed quickly, and with an economy of effort which suggests he has been doing the same thing for a number of years, including hitting his heads every morning. Performing the next few moves he remains doubled-up to avoid further accident. Holding his head with one hand he reaches for his robe with the other, in the meantime stopping into a pair of slippers. Once donned, the robe gives testimony of a former and larger owner. Now heading to the side of the room where the stove is located, he accommodates his walk to the height of the ceiling, starting our in a semi-crouch and straightening up as the ceiling gets higher.

This is a walk he uses habitually in his room. As he reaches the stove, he moves the kettle off the burner, and the SOUND STOPS. Squeegee then stands a minute, waking up. He does a few abortive knee bends, takes a couple of not-too-deep breaths, and is ready to face the day. Starting briskly on his morning routine, he walks back near the bed, straightens it superficially, then returns to the crib.

TIGHTER ANGLE—AT CRIB

As Squeegee smiles down. He extends a finger for a quick tickle, and then goes to the drawer of a battered dresser and takes out a small hair ribbon, matches the color scheme against the dress, and is satisfied.

CLOSE SHOT—SQUEEGEE

As he loans over the crib smiling and clucking all the while, he dresses the occupant quickly.

WIDER ANGLE

He then returns to the gas burner, taking some child's dishes and utensils out of a cabinet beneath the stove. From another cabinet he takes a small glass of orange juice, and pours another small glass full of milk. He puts a small skillet on the burner, puts some butter in it, takes out an egg carton and finds it empty. He goes to the window, opens it, and comes face to face with:

CLOSE SHOT—ON WINDOW LEDGE

A large, black, truculent-looking pigeon. He sits there defiantly.

WIDER ANGLE

To include Squeegee. He attempts to shoo it away with his hand, and gets pecked for his pains. He goes back to the food cabinet beneath the stove and gets out a large dill pickle. He goes back to the window, and offers the pickle to the pigeon. The pigeon pecks at the pickle tentatively and Squeegee slides his hand beneath the bird and brings out a large hen's egg. He puts the pickle down and the pigeon walks over to it.

CLOSE SHOT—LEDGE

It can be seen that the pigeon was sitting on a portion of an egg carton, holding three eggs. This is Squeegee's outdoor storage space.

FULL SHOT—ROOM

Squeegee takes the egg back to the stove, polishing it on his sleeve. He cracks it into the skillet, stirring it a few times with a fork. While it is cooking, he pulls out a child's high chair and puts all the food on the tray. Now he takes a date from a box and then goes over to the crib.

CLOSE SHOT—AT CRIB

As Squeegee's hands lift the occupant into view. Clad in the child's dress, appealingly bedecked with the bow, is a tiny ring-tailed monkey. Her name is Paulette and, as we shall soon learn, she is a kleptomaniac.

TWO SHOT—SQUEEGEE AND PAULETTE

As Squeegee holds the monkey they exchange looks of complete adoration. Squeegee gives Paulette her special morning favor, the date.

CLOSE SHOT—PAULETTE

She quickly ears the date, then spits out the pit.

CLOSE SHOT—SQUEEGEE

He holds his eye, where the pit got him.

FULL SHOT—ROOM

Holding his eye, Squeegee takes Paulette over to the high chair, sears here, and motions for her to eat her breakfast. Paulette takes up her knife and fork, and Squeegee watches her fondly. He then remembers the egg, makes a dive for it and gets it off the stove just in time. He serves Paulette the egg.

CLOSE SHOT—PAULETTE

She reacts to the egg, not altogether favorably.

WIDER ANGLE

Squeegee looks at the clock, reacts, then goes to the shower curtain, and takes off his robe. He starts to pull his nightshirt over his head, and then looks back at Paulette.

CLOSE SHOT—PAULETTE

She makes a face at Squeegee, then covers her eyes.

FULL SHOT—ROOM

Squeegee smiles back, modestly goes around in back of the shower curtain and enters from the rear. The nightshirt comes up over the top of the curtain and falls to the floor.

CLOSE SHOT—PAULETTE

She looks at the egg and makes another face. Turning in her chair she looks off towards window.

CLOSE SHOT—WINDOW LEDGE

The pigeon waits expectantly.

FULL SHOT—ROOM

Paulette climbs out of her high chair, takes the plate with the egg and offers it to the pigeon.

CLOSE SHOT—WINDOW LEDGE

The pigeon makes short shrift of the egg, while Paulette shoots anxious glances back towards shower curtain.

WIDER ANGLE

The pigeon is finished. Hastily, Paulette snatches the plate and runs back to her high chair, climbs into place, and puts her empty plate in front of her, just as the shower curtains part.

MED. CLOSE SHOT—AT SHOWER

Squeegee parts the curtain and steps through. He is completely dressed. As he steps out, it is seen that Squeegee has his dressing room inside the shower curtain for the sake of modesty. His clothes are neat, but about thirty years too late. CAMERA FOLLOWS him to the high chair, where he bends over to inspect Paulette's plate. He smiles happily at the empty plate, and Paulette stealthily lifts his watch out of his vest pocket. As he straightens up, patting her on the head, he sees her with the watch. He shakes his finger in reproof, and takes the watch back. He then tidies her face with a napkin, and lifts her out of the high chair. He takes his wallet from his breast pocket and puts it in his back pocket, takes a tightly-rolled umbrella and puts it jauntily over his arm, and puts on his hat. With Paulette perched on his arm, he moves to the door. He then stops and locks down.

CLOSE SHOT—FLOOR

A paper has been thrust under the door. Squeegee's hand picks it up.

NSERT—PAPER

It is a rent statement. The words, "Rent Due", are clearly visible.

MED. SHOT—AT DOOR

Squeegee reaches in his back pocket for his wallet. It is not there. He looks around. Paulette has taken it out of his pocket while he was bending over. He takes it from her, and shakes his finger at her in a scolding way. He peeks into the wallet, returns it to his pocket, and starts to go. He stops at a sign posted on the inside of the door.

INSERT—SIGN

It is a list of rules, printed in single lines. They are: "No smoking. No drinking. No guests. No cooking. No children. NO PETS."

BACK TO SCENE

Squeegee picks up Paulette and stows her away inside his coat.

CLOSE SHOT—PAULETTE

She emerges to give the sign the raspberry.

MED. SHOT—AT DOOR

Squeegee takes several peanuts from his pocket, gives them to Paulette, and gently pushes her back inside his coat. He opens the deer cautiously.

MED. SHOT—HALL

Squeegee's head comes through the door, looks around. Satisfied, he emerges, closes his door, and starts down the hall, looking over his shoulder. CAMERA DOLLIES WITH HIM. As Squeegee turns to face front, he finds himself face to face with the landlord, a large, suspicious man dressed in pants and vest, but no coat. His shirt sleeves are rolled up, exposing the long underwear beneath. Squeegee smiles nervously, tips his hat, and sidesteps to get around the landlord. The landlord steps with him, blocking his path. He produces another rent statement from his pocket and thrusts it at Squeegee. Squeegee sidesteps again and the landlord steps with him. The movements of the landlord are unhurried, but he easily blocks the narrow hall. Squeegee now pretends to understand, and reaches in his inside coat pocket for his wallet, which of course is in his hip pocket. As he is fumbling, the landlord loans in closer to see what is going on.

CLOSE SHOT—LANDLORD

A handful of peanut shells magically hit him in the face and he straightens up suddenly. He glares at Squeegee.

CLOSE SHOT—SQUEEGEE

He smiles weakly — shows that his hands were occupied elsewhere.

MED. SHOT — HALL

Squeegee now reaches into his hip pocket and produces his wallet. He takes out the slender amount of bills, counting them out carefully onto the wallet, which is flat in his hand. He then takes the bills, folds them if half, and with a little bow hands the tattered wallet to the landlord while returning the bills to his pocket, all with one motion. At the same time he steps around the landlord, tips his hat, and is gone down the hall.

CLOSE SHOT — LANDLORD

He does a very slight landlord's smile as he looks down the hall after Squeegee, then slowly looks down at the wallet in his hand. Furious, he throws the wallet down on the floor.

QUICK DISSOLVE:

FULL SHOT — STREET SCENE — DAY — (STOCK)

A busy New York street scene is established.

DISSOLVE:

CLOSE SHOT — STREET SIGN

It is a sign indicating the intersection of Broad and Wall Streets.

DISSOLVE:

FULL SHOT — SKYSSCRAPER (STOCK)

CAMERA SWEEPS DOWN side of skyscraper.

DISSOLVE:

FULL SHOT — ELEVATOR ENTRANCE (IN LOBBY)

A number of people are entering an elevator. Squeegee flies into the scene and barely makes it as the doors close.

MED. SHOT — INT. ELEVATOR

CAMERA IS SHOOTING toward rear of elevator. Squeegee is somehow thrust against the back wall of the car. The operator looks around as the people in the crowded car call out their floors, and he punches the corresponding buttons on his board. Those calling their floors are a far businessman smoking a cigar, a large and bosomy matron, a Brinks guard carrying a moneybag strapped to his wrist, a delivery boy carrying a parcel, a foreign-looking financier with a mustache, who speaks with a Spanish accent, and Skinner, a broker Squeegee meets later in the day. In addition, Skinner's partner Selby is in the car, along with the beautiful secretary of the firm...both of whom figure in the later action. There is also a legal-looking man with a briefcase.

>
WOMAN
>BUSINESSMAN
>BRINKS GUARD
>FINANCIER
>SKINNER
>DELIVERY BOY
>LAWYER

>SQUEEGEE

Basement.

All stare at him.

>BUSINESSMAN
>(impatiently)

Why can't you walk down? It's only one flight.

>OPERATOR

I'll drop you on the way down.

>SQUEEGEE
>(mildly)

Well — if it's net out of your way.

The operator gives him a look, and starts the car upward. The occupants look straight ahead, having that uncomfortable elevator look. Squeegee is standing next to the stout matron. As Paulette chest assumes the shelf-like appearance of the matron. She looks at him, sure that he is making fun of her in some way she can't quite figure out. Squeegee shrugs helplessly, and slightly holds out both hands to indicate his innocence. She faces front again stiffly, then looks back at Squeegee in some amazement. Paulette has now worked around to back. His coat is undulating gently. Squeegee repents the gesture with the hands. The matron edges away from him, and the financier with the mustache is now close to Squeegee. He takes a look as the end of Paulette's tail is now under Squeegee's nose, as sore of a burlesque mustache. Squeegee holds up his hands. The financier looks away, then back as the tail disappears. Squeegee is unaware of its being gone, and twirls the non-existent mustache. Squeegee looks down, smiles uncomfortably, and then gives his cost a small pat to quiet Paulette. He can't locate her, and turns around to see where she is. During this he works his way towards the front of the car. Everyone looks to see what he is searching for, including the operator.

CLOSE SHOT—SQUEEGEE'S BACK

A hairy hand comes out of his coat collar at the neck and depresses THE EMERGENCY STOP BUTTON: The car stops abruptly.

The fat businessman with the cigar is looking down as the doors open. He walks out, crashing into the blank wall in front of him and smashing the cigar back against his face. The car has stopped between floors. The man looks in pain and anger at the operator.

> OPERATOR
> Very sorry, Sir.

He closes the doors and starts the car, looking hard at his board.

CLOSE SHOT—FLOOR INDICATOR

The light flashes 40, 41, 42, 43, 44, 45, 46, and stops at 47.

MED. SHOT—ELEVATOR

> OPERATOR
> (looking up)
> Forty-seven.

> BUSINESSMAN
> (irate)
> What happened to forty-one?

> OPERATOR
> Sorry, Sir, Get you on the way down.

He opens the doors, and the lawyer with the briefcase starts to get out. Squeegee moves aside to make room for him, and as he turns the crook of his umbrella hooks the back of the lawyer's collar. As he walks out Squeegee feels his umbrella begin to go, and yanks it back. The lawyer, halfway out of the car, comes sailing back. His briefcase describes an are and whacks the operator, causing him to close the door. Everyone glares around, not quite sure what is happening. The operator stares hard at his board before starting the car up again, and while he is doing so Paulette's hand comes out of Squeegee's coat and lifts the financier's watch. He feels for it just as Squeegee takes it away from Paulette. The financier looks at him, and Squeegee hands him the watch. The financier grabs it and advances toward Squeegee threateningly. Squeegee backs away hastily. In the meantime the operator, not seeing what is going on behind him, has stopped the car and opened the doors.

As the woman starts to get out, Squeegee backs into the control board, and the tip of his umbrella hits one of the buttons. The doors close in the woman's face, and the elevator starts up again. The operator is baffled.

> FINANCIER
> Arrest that man:

> OPERATOR
> I wish I could.

The suspicious financier glares at Squeegee and takes out his wallet and starts checking his money. A Brinks armed guard is standing in front of him with a bag of money strapped to his wrist.

CLOSE SHOT—MONEY BAG

Paulette's hand enters the scene and starts to pull in the money bag.

FULL SHOT—ELEVATOR

The guard feels the pull and jerks the bag back. He turns and sees the financier with the money in his hand, seemingly in the act of putting it in his wallet. He grabs the money from the financier. A general melee starts. The elevator stops and the door opens. Trying to see what is going on, the operator catches a fist in the eye and catapults out through the door. Squeegee backs away from struggle. Paulette's hand emerges again, and the doors shut and the elevator starts down. There is a general clamor of people wanting to get out. As Squeegee is now standing where the operator was, the clamor is directed to him. He presses a button, and the car stops with extreme suddenness. The passengers are thrown into a heap on the floor. Squeegee bows a polite apology, and his umbrella hits another button, starting the car down again. All get up, glaring at him.

CLOSE SHOW—FLOOR INDICATOR

The numbers flow by rapidly, slowing when they approach the ground floor. The lights finally flash, "Basement."

FULL SHOT—ELEVATOR

The car stops and the door opens. The crowd parts silently to make room for Squeegee, regarding him with loathing. He backs out, smiling his apologies. The point of his umbrella almost jabs the "FINANCIER" in the stomach. He stops it with his hand. Squeegee turns, again apologizing with his smile, and goes out, the creek of his umbrella catching the FINANCIER across the eyes.

WIPE:

CLOSE SHOT—GLASS DOOR

It reads, "Sunshine Building Maintenance."

                                                        DISSOLVE THROUGH:

MED. SHOT—LOCKER ROOM

Squeegee enters, steps in front of his locker, and brings Paulette cut from under his coat, seating her on top of the locker row. He then takes out a large key ring, clips a fingernail with a small clippers on the ring, puts the keys away and opens his locker, which was unlocked. As Paulette watches, he takes out a polo mallet, tries a few swings, puts it away and takes out a pool cue. After several dry run shots, he puts this away and takes out a bucket and squeegee. He then strips off his outer clothes, exposing his work coveralls beneath. He is hanging up his other clothes as Virgil approaches, a clipboard in hand. Virgil is the maintenance dispatcher, around thirty-five smallish, with a know-it-all attitude.

                    VIRGIL
                 (checks board)
           Morning, Squeegee. How's Paulette?

                   SQUEEGEE
              She's very dishonest.

CLOSE SHOT—PAULETTE

She makes a face, hops down alongside Virgil.

MED. SHOT—LOCKER ROOM

Virgil looks at Paulette closely, as a doctor would.

                    VIRGIL
             Kleptomania!

                   SQUEEGEE
          Huh?

                    VIRGIL
           Compulsive stealing, Squeegee, that
           Monkey needs help.

SQUEEGEE
Oh no — she works fast enough alone! In the elevator she stole...

VIRGIL
No, no, no! I mean therapy, She's a neurotic thief.

SQUEEGEE
(defensively)
She only steals from the rich and gives to the poor.

VIRGIL
Robin Hood complex. My uncle had it. But it can be cured.

SQUEEGEE
What did they give him for it?

VIRGIL
Five years. I warn you that monkey'll wind up in the clink.

CLOSE SHOT — PAULETTE

She quickly holds out Virgil's watch, which she has pinched. Her face has a very contrite expression.

MED. SHOT — LOCKER ROOM

Virgil takes the watch.

SQUEEGEE
(weak laugh)
She's just passing the time.

VIRGIL
Get her to a good animal psychiatrist. Talk it out.

SQUEEGEE
How can you talk to a monkey?

Virgil is impatient with such ignorance.

VIRGIL
Psychiatrists don't talk, they listen.

SQUEEGEE
(satisfied)
Oh.

VIRGIL
I'll see if I can locate a cheap one by the time you get through.

SQUEEGEE
Where am I working today, Virgil?

VIRGIL
(looks at board)
Seventy-sixth floor.

SQUEEGEE
How come I never get to go out? Fourteen years, all I wash is Wall Street.

VIRGIL
Well you can always tell people you clean up in the market.

He laughs, but Squeegee shows no appreciation.

SQUEEGEE
Very funny! Yesterday a guy with half my seniority gets sent to a girls' college.

                    VIRGIL
You're too susceptible. 76th floor. And
take your safety belt.

He takes it out of his locker and hands it to him.

                    SQUEEGEE
I can't use it. Makes me nervous.

He puts it back in the locker. Paulette chatters. Squeegee looks at her, then at Virgil. Virgil knows what is coming.

                    SQUEEGEE
Could you...?

                    VIRGIL
No!

                    SQUEEGEE
Just this morning?

                    VIRGIL
Take her with you!

                    SQUEEGEE
She can't stand heights.

                    VIRGIL
I can't stand her!

                    SQUEEGEE
She likes you.

                    VIRGIL
What am I? A monkeysitter?
                    (weakening)
Besides, she won't behave.

Paulette jumps down and runs off.

          SQUEEGEE
Yes, she will, Virgil. Just play with her.
Look, she's ready to play,

CLOSE SHOT—PAULETTE

She is sitting at a table, dealing cards.

CLOSE SHOT—VIRGIL

He reacts violently.

FULL SHOT—LOCKER ROOM

          VIRGIL
How do you play gin with a monkey?

          SQUEEGEE
Regular way. The cards a piece, loser
deals, double for spades.

          VIRGIL
You must be angry.

Squeegee picks up his equipment and gets ready to depart.

          SQUEEGEE
I think you can bear her if she doesn't cheat.

CLOSE SHOT—PAULETTE

She gives a dishonest look, takes an ace out of her dress, replaces it in deck.

TWO SHOT—VIRGIL AND SQUEEGEE

They both react and Squeegee exits shaking his head.

                            DISSOLVE:

CLOSE SHOT—OFFICE DOOR

It is lettered, "Skinner and Selby, Investment Brokers, 7602."

DISSOLVE THROUGH:

FULL SHOT—OFFICE RECEPTION ROO

The beautiful secretary, seen earlier in the elevator, is at a desk when Squeegee comes in. He shuts the door behind him. She pays no attention to him, reading a fashion magazine. He starts past her desk, looks, and is obviously overwhelmed. He clears his threat. Without looking up, she gestures toward the inner office. He steps at the door to the inner office, and is slowly drawn back.

CLOSE SHOT—SECRETARY

She continues to look at the page of the magazine. Squeegee's head comes into the picture, looking over her shoulder. She turns, and his face is an inch from hers. He smiles, and raises his hat. She looks right through him. He straightens up. She looks back at the picture, and sighs.

TWO SHOT—SQUEEGEE AND SECRETARY

He looks to see what she is sighing at.

INSERT—MAGAZINE PAGE

A model is wearing a full-length mink coat.

TWO SHOT—SQUEEGEE AND SECRETARY

She sighs over the coat again. Squeegee pulls his slender roll of bills out of his pocket, and counts them. He has four dollars. He looks to see the price of the coat.

INSERT—MAGAZINE PAGE

The secretary removes her hand from the bottom of the page, showing the price. It is fifteen hundred dollars.

FULL SHOT—RECEPTION ROOM

Squeegee sadly returns his four dollars to his pocket. He goes into the inner office, looking back, and the secretary continues to look at the coat.

FULL SHOT—INTERIOR OFFICE

The office has a long board table on one side and a market ticker on the other. Skinner and Selby, two avaricious types seen earlier in the elevator, pay no attention as Squeegee walks in. Selby is checking the ticker and Skinner is seated at the table, going through the Wall St, Journal. Squeegee walks between them to the window.

> SELBY
> (looking at ticker)
> Your hot special on Middle East. Oil went down another two points.

> SKINEER
> Selby, we've get to make a killing!

> SELBY
> (glances at him)
> I think I'd like to.

By this time Squeegee is at the window, and has opened it. The secretary enters the room from the reception room and goes to a filing cabinet.

MED. CLOSE SHOT—AT WINDOW

Squeegee, looking back at the secretary, steps out of the window without looking, and drops from sight.

LONG VIEW—EXT. BUILDING (PROCESS)

Looking down into the street for below, only Squeegee's hands are visible, holding onto the ledge. To then see his feet kicking.

FULL SHOT—INT. OFFICE

Skinner looks slowly at the window, puzzled.

> SKINNER
> (to Selby)
> Did a man just come through here and jump cut the window?

Selby looks at him.

> SELBY
> I've seen this coming... you're out of your mind.

MED. SHOT—EXT. BUILDING

Squeegee has gotten a log over the edge, and hoists himself up. Upright again, he dusts himself off as it nothing had happened, and reaches down for his squeegee and bucket.

CLOSE SHOT—SKINNER

He is wondering if he really has lost his mind. He stares at the window.

CLOSE SHOT—WINDOW—SKINNER'S PV

Squeegee rises into view, splashing water on the window and then wiping it off with the squeegee.

FULL SHOT—OFFICE

Skinner opens his mouth to call Selby's attention to his vindication. Squeegee, outside the window, bends over again, out of view. Skinner decides to keep quiet, and hastily looks down to his papers.

DISSOLVE:

MED. SHOT—EXT. BUILDING

It is several hours later. Squeegee is finishing the exterior of a window lettered "Peru Platinum, Ltd." After a finishing flourish, he lowers the window and straddles it in order to do the inside.

FULL SHOT—INT. OFFICE

This is an office much like the Skinner and Selby office. A number of Latin-looking men are sitting around a board table. There is a conspiratorial air, and they seem about to come to a decision. One of them holds up his hand for a halt, and rises. It is the mustached financier from the elevator.

>   FINANCIER
>   Memento.

He goes to the two office doors, checking them to make sure no one is listening outside. He goes to a desk and makes sure the intercom is turned off, then comes back to the table.

>   FINANCIER
>   We are agreed, then?

There is a general, hushed chorus of "Si." The financier picks up the phone on the table.

>   FINANCIER
>   (into phone, hushed)
>   Get me Roberto at the Exchange floor.
>
>   (pause)
>   Roberto? We have decided. No merger.
>   Wait till a few minutes before the market
>   closes. Then... sell!

He hangs up, permitting himself a smile. The others smile, and there is a figurative rubbing of hands. Squeegee finishes the window and steps out, still with me one paying any attention to him.

MED. SHOT—EXT. BUILDING

Squeegee closes the window and takes off down the ledge, CAMERA FOLLOWING. He pauses to wipe a speck off a window with his elbow. The window is lettered, " Consolidated Asphalt." He peers in very briefly, then continues down the ledge. At the window of Skinner and Selby, he looks in, but apparently does not see the secretary. The NOON WHISTLE BLOWS. Squeegee sits down on the ledge, dangling his feet over the edge.

LONG VIEW—STREET TRAFFIC BELOW (PROCESS)

MED. SHOT—LEDGE

Squeegee takes a small tablecloth from his pocket and spreads it on the ledge beside him. He then takes food and utensils from his other pockets, setting the table nearly. He lays out a varied assortment of foods from cartons produced from different pockets, sprinkling a little salt on a salad from a small paper container. He is just about to eat when the large black pigeon seen earlier flies up and perches on the ledge.

SQUEEGEE
You're almost late to lunch, Randolph.

He takes a large drill pickle out of his pocket and places it on the ledge for Randolph. As he is ready to start his lunch again, a cloud of other pigeons descend on the ledge. Squeegee tries to shoo them off, but to no avail. They finally take off again.

CLOSE SHOT—TABLECLOTH

The table is completely bare, except for the small salt shaker.

MED. SHOT—LEDGE

Squeegee looks at Randolph rather bitterly.

SQUEEGEE
Did you have to invite friends?

One pigeon returns, picks up the sale shaker, and flies off again. Squeegee shrugs, gets up and opens the Skinner and Selby window, starting in.

FULL SHOT—OFFICE

Skinner and Selby are in a heated, table-pounding argument. Squeegee is climbing in the window.

SKINNER
You idiot, you're passing up millions!

SELBY
(sitting back)
I say you don't know what you're talking about.

SKINNER
It's inevitable! Peru Platinum has to merge! The stock will skyrocket:

SELBY
I still don't understand what Bended debentures have to do with a merger!

SKINNER
(burning up)
You know less about the market then this window washer!

He indicates Squeegee, who is crossing the room, Squeegee stops.

SELBY
I do? Then ask him about Peru Platinum!

SKINNER
I will!

(to Squeegee)
You!

SQUEEGEE
No?

SKINNER
If you had money, would you buy Peru Platinum?

SQUEEGEE
(negative)
Uh-uh.

SELBY
(triumphant)
See!

SKINNER
          Stupid! That's why he's a window cleaner!

                    SQUEEGEE
          The stock should drop around eight
          points before the market closes today.

Skinner and Selby stare.

                    SKINNER
                    (shouts)
          Stocks don't drop when companies
          merge...

                    SQUEEGEE
          They won't merge. Now if you want
          something good...

                    SKINNER
                    (against his will)
          What?

Squeegee looks around.

                    SQUEEGEE
          Consolidated Asphalt. Big government
          contract. It should be good for ten points.

                    SKINNER
                    (supreme scorn)
          I will personally eat every pound of
          asphalt they sell to the government and
          you are a nitwit!

Squeegee doesn't seem to hear him. He walks up to Skinner, looking at him closely. He then whips out a clean handkerchief, rubs a spot off Skinner's glasses, and goes out, leaving the two staring after him.

FULL SHOT—RECEPTION ROOM

Squeegee comes in, closing the door from the outer office. The secretary is not in the room, but he notices the fashion magazine open on her desk. After looking around, he picks it up and tears out the page containing the illustration of the coat. He is going out as the secretary comes in. He hastily puts the page behind him. She stares at him curiously. He tries to back out the door, and in his confusion backs into the water cooler.

CLOSE SHOT—SQUEEGEE

He turns and catches the top of the water cooler just as it is about to tip over. The bottom frame crashes, but he catches the bottle. He turns proudly to the secretary.

> SQUEEGEE
> Got it!

FULL SHOT—RECEPTION ROOM

He sees her looking down, and follows her gaze. The contents of the upside-down bottle are running all over his pants and shoes.

CLOSE SHOT—SQUEEGEE

He smiles his embarrassed smile.

> DISSOLVE:

FULL SHOT—LOCKER ROOM

Virgil is seated, playing cards with Paulette as Squeegee enters, dripping.

> VIRGIL
> Railing out?

> SQUEEGEE
> (DISREGARDING THIS)
> Virgil, you think the company would give me a salary advance?

                    VIRGIL
        How much?

While he is looking around at Squeegee, Paulette crawls over the table, attempting to get a look at his hand. He holds his cards up closer, without looking at her.

                    SQUEEGEE
        Fifteen hundred dollars.

                    VIRGIL
        That's a pretty big advance.

                    SQUEEGEE
        I have to buy a girl a mink coat.

He sits down and takes off his dripping shoes.

                    VIRGIL
        You're engaged?

                    SQUEEGEE
        Not exactly.

                    VIRGIL
        What's her name?

                    SQUEEGEE
        I don't know.

                    VIRGIL
        She is a girl?

Squeegee pours the water out of one shoe.

                    SQUEEGEE
        She's gorgeous.

> **VIRGIL**
> Fifteen hundred dollars. How much you have now?

> **SQUEEGEE**
> Four dollars. But I owe the landlord eight.

> **VIRGIL**
> You think a mink coat is practical?

As Squeegee takes off his other shoe, Paulette runs over, takes the shoe, and hops up on the bench beside him.

> **SQUEEGEE**
> She's the most beautiful thing in the world.

Paulette, out of jealousy, empties the water-filled shoe over his head.

CUT TO:

FULL SHOT—SELBY AND SKINNER OFFICE

Selby is at the ticker, Skinner is pacing up and down, looking at his watch. The secretary is at the filing cabinet.

> **SKINNER**
> Three o'clock. I tell you we should have put every cent into Peru Platinum! The market will be closing, and we missed the boat!

> **SELBY**
> (looking at tape)
> It hasn't moved a point.

> **SKINNER**
> It hasn't gone down, has it? Wait till they announce the merger!

SELBY

Rumors.

SKINNER

Go believe an idiot window washer! We could have been rich!

Selby looks at the tape, then beckons Skinner.

SELBY

Quick — a flash on Peru!

Skinner comes over.

SKINNER
(reading)

No...merger?

SELBY

The bottom is dropping out.

SKINNER

How did he know?

SELBY
(reading)

Company announced decision — spokesman indicated liabilities — last sale Peru Platinum — block of 10,000 Shares... **DOWN EIGHT POINTS:**

SKINNER
(in amazement)

That's what he said...eight points. That stupid dolt!

SELBY

Quick! What was the name of that other stock?...the one he said would go up?

> SKINNER
> Consolidated Asphalt... ten points.

Selby checks the tape frantically, practically pulling it out of the machine.

> SELBY
> Here it is... they're building airstrips for the government in Africa... it went from eighty to ninety!

> SKINNER
> Ten points... but how did he Know? That ignorant lout!

> SELBY
> Who cares? He must be psychic.
> (to secretary)
> Find that man! The window cleaner! Call the maintenance company!

> SECRETARY
> Yes sir.

She goes to the phone quickly.

> SELBY
> This man is worth millions to us... billions! We've got to get him!

Skinner is still shaking his head.

> SECRETARY
> (from phone)
> He's gone home for the day, Mr. Selby.

> SELBY
> Find out where he lives! We'll go there!

                    SECRETARY
            Yes sir.

                    SKINNER
            (beginning to see the vision)
            Why, we could corner the market!

                    SELBY
            Corner the market? We'll corner the
            country! Think big, Skinner! We'll corner
            the world!

                    SKINNER
            (with fierce pride)
            And to think that I discovered him.

As Selby reacts,

                                                FADE OUT

FADE IN:

FULL SHOT—HALLWAY OF ROOMING HOUSE—DAY

Squeegee comes down the hallway, holding Paulette beneath his coat. He stops in front of the door of his room, turns the knob, and starts to go in. As the door remains shut, he walks right into it. He rubs his injured nose reflectively, then gets out his large bunch of keys. Selecting one with care, he puts it into the lock, turns it, and again walks into the door. He then bends over for a closer look.

CLOSE SHOT—DOOR

A large padlock has been freshly attached to the door.

CLOSE SHOT—SQUEEGEE

He reacts to the padlock. Paulette sticks her head out, sees the padlock, and gives it the raspberry. She ducks back in again.

FULL SHOT—HALLWAY

The landlord is standing directly behind Squeegee, slapping the dilapidated wallet into his hand. Squeegee slowly straightens up and faces him. He tries a smile.

> SQUEEGEE
> The door... seems to be locked.

> LANDLORD
> Eight dollars.

> SQUEEGEE
> I'm a little short. You see, I'm saving up to buy a mink coat.

> LANDLORD
> You'll need it. Out!

He gestures down the hall. Squeegee attempts a weak bluster.

> SQUEEGEE
> Now just a minute, innkeeper!

He reaches inside his coat pocket and fumbles around. The landlord leans over. The dose of peanut shells hits him in the eye. He straightens up.

> LANDLORD
> Out! Now!

> SKINNER'S VOICE
> (c.s.)
> There he is! That's him!

Squeegee and the landlord look down the hall as Skinner and Selby rush up, grabbing on to Squeegee like a lost son, and shoving the landlord aside.

> SELBY
> My boy!

SKINNER
It happened!

SQUEEGEE
What happened?

SKINNER
The stocks! Just what you said! How did you know?

SQUEEGEE
(reflecting)
I really couldn't say.

SELBY
But you know? About other stocks?

SQUEEGEE
Of course.

SKINNER
That's good enough! You're working for us!

The landlord tries to reassert his position.

LANDLORD
What about my eight dollars?

All ignore him.

SQUEEGEE
But I've got a job.

SELBY
Forget it!

SKINNER
You'll be our partner! We'll make millions!

SQUEEGEE
I don't think I need that much.

LANDLORD
What about my eight dollars?

SELBY
(again ignoring the landlord)
Of course you need money, my boy. Everyone does. Think what you could do with a million.

SQUEEGEE
I could use fifteen hundred.

SKINNER
You'll make it in five minutes!

LANDLORD
He owes me eight dollars!

SKINNER
Take twenty and go away.

He airily hands him a bill. The landlord takes it, dazed.

SELBY
(to Squeegee)
That wasn't for rent?

As Squeegee nods, Selby tears the bill out of the landlord's hand.

SELBY
You won't be needing this batroost... you're coming with us!

SQUEEGEE
But this is my home.

SKINNER
Our home is your home! We love you!
Until the market opens in the morning,
we won't let you out of our sight!

                     SELBY
Some clothes, dinner, night club... we'll
make a night of it!

                   SQUEEGEE
Will your... secretary be there?

Skinner catches a quick signal from Selby.

                    SKINNER
Of course she will! She loves you too!

This convinces Squeegee.

                   LANDLORD
But my eight dollars?

                     SELBY
Send us your statement.

                    SKINNER
One side, ruffian!

They thrust him against the wall, and take hold of Squeegee on either side.

CLOSE SHOT—LANDLORD

As Squeegee passes, the peanut shells come out of the back of his collar, taking him in the face. The landlord looks after them as they go off, looks at the wallet still in his hand, and slams it down on the floor.

                                          DISSOLVE:

FULL SHOT—NIGHT CLUB—NIGHT

Skinner, Squeegee, the Secretary, and Selby are seated in that order at a small table, facing CAMERA. Skinner and Selby are both in evening dress, and the Secretary wears an evening gown which shows her off to best advantage. Squeegee is in tails which are obviously rented. All wear paper hats, here are noisemakers and champagne coolers on the table, and Skinner and Selby are celebrating with most of the stops out. The girl is rather bored, looking around for a more exciting male acquaintance than Squeegee, who is almost prostrate with shyness. A paper streamer is thrown from another table, and Skinner stands up and hurls a streamer back. He is in high spirits, and wants to pour Squeegee a drink of champagne.

> SKINNER
> Champagne, my boy! Tomorrow we own
> the world!

Squeegee holds his hand over his glass.

> SQUEEGEE
> I never drink, really. It affects my work.

> SELBY
> But you're working for us!

> SQUEEGEE
> I don't think I'd better. And it's past my
> bedtime.

Selby nudges the Secretary, who gets the signal. She turns the charm on Squeegee.

> SECRETARY
> Won't you drink a toast with me?

> SQUEEGEE
> (melts)
> Why not?

Skinner fills the glasses, and they raise them in toast.

       SKINNER
    To the first million!

They drink.

CLOSE SHOT—SQUEEGEE

He takes a large gulp, then reacts with a dazed look as the explosion takes place inside.

FULL SHOT—TABLE

The others watch Squeegee's reaction as he slowly puts his glass down. There are visible movements inside his coat has Paulette signals for a drink. The others stare as Squeegee pulls out his vest and pours the small remaining portion of his drink into the aperture. He sees the others looking at him, and seemingly rubs the champagne in.

       SQUEEGEE
   Wine for the stomach's sake.

CLOSE SHOT—TABLE

A small hand reaches out from Squeegee's vest and drags in a noisemaker.

FULL SHOT—TABLE

The others look on in amazement as the noisemaker suddenly unrolls across the table with a whistling sound, propelled by the invisible Paulette from inside Squeegee's vest. Squeegee taps his lower chest politely.

       SQUEEGEE
    Something I ate.

The noisemaker repeats, to Squeegee's embarrassment. To distract attention, he throws a streamer with one hand and with a lightning move with the other whisks Paulette out of his coat and under the table. He looks around blandly as the others stare, not sure just what happened.

CLOSE SHOT—UNDER TABLE

Paulette looks around at the legs, not sure where to start operations.

FULL SHOT—TABLE

      SQUEEGEE
     (to the Secretary)
  Dance?

She shakes her head. She then feels something under the table. Paulette has started operations. The Secretary jumps a little bit and looks at Squeegee, who feigns ignorance. She jumps again and looks at Selby: He makes the mistake of giving her a big smile.

      SECRETARY
  Mr. Selby!

She cracks him a good one, getting up. Selby is bewildered.

      SECRETARY
     (to Squeegee)
  Dance?

He gets up, delighted. Skinner looks at Selby accusingly, but he doesn't know what it is all about.

FULL SHOT—DANCE FLOOR

The orchestra is playing a mambo, o.s. Squeegee goes into an exaggerated version of the dance and soon has the floor cleared but for himself and his partner. At the height of his success, he spins the Secretary away from. As she twirls, a handsome young man steps on the floor and takes her in his arms. At this moment the music changes to something slow and romantic, and the young man and the secretary dance off. Squeegee, left standing by the table, sits down wordlessly, looking. Skinner fills his glass with champagne and he drinks it, still looking off.

FADE OUT

FADE IN:

CLOSE SHOT—SQUEEGEE

Only his head is visible, with a monstrous ice bag resting on top of it, and almost covering it. His eyes are closed.

CAMERA PULLS BACK FOR:

FULL SHOT—SELBY AND SKINNER OFFICE—DAY

Selby and Skinner are looking anxiously at Squeegee. All three still have their evening clothes on, having made a night of it.

SKINNER

Is he alive?

SELBY

I don't know.

He lifts up the ice bag, and looks at Squeegee.

SKINNER
(helpfully)

He's breathing.

SELBY

Why did you give him all that champagne last night?

SKINNER

He didn't even get the second glass down.

(to Squeegee)

Wake up.

Selby looks at his watch.

                    SELBY
        The market opens in two minutes.

The Secretary appears in the door. She is wearing her working clothes.

                    SKINNER
        Tomato juice!

                    SECRETARY
        Yes, Mr. Skinner.

She exits again. Squeegee groans.

                    SELBY
        He's coming to!

                    SKINNER
              (not wasting a moment)
        What do you think of Farnsworth
        Mattress?

Selby starts massaging Squeegee's palms.

                    SELBY
        United Zinc?

Squeegee opens his eyes as the Secretary comes back with the voice. He takes it from her and drinks it, then pours the last few drips down the aperture in his vest for Paulette.

                    SKINNER
        International Tractor.

Squeegee staggers to his feet. The door opens and a painter comes in, with a bucket and brushes. Selby rushes over to him.

                    SELBY
          No, no! Come back later!

He pushes the man out the door. He leaves his bucket behind. Squeegee weaves over.

                   SKINNER
         Farnsworth Mattress! Up or down?

Operating on sense memory, Squeegee takes the bucket and goes over to the open window, starting to step out. Skinner and Selby rush after him and grab him as he is halfway out the window.

                    SELBY
          No, no! You're with us now!

They drag him back in the room.

                   SKINNER
            Farnsworth mattress?

Squeegee gets himself into focus.

                  SQUEEGEE
             Uh-uh.

                    SELBY
                (to Skinner)
          See? You never could pick a stock.
                (to Squeegee)
             United Zinc?

                  SQUEEGEE
             Buy.

                    SELBY
                (to Secretary)
          Phone that in! Five thousand shares!

> SKINNER
> International tractor?

> SQUEEGEE
> Uh-uh.

> SELBY
> General Oatmeal.

> SQUEEGEE
> Buy.

> SELBY
> (excited, to Secretary)
> Get that? Same order!
>
> (to Skinner)
> Check the ticker!

As the secretary remains on the phone, Skinner goes to the ticker. Squeegee sinks down in a chair as Selby goes through the Journal.

> SKINNER
> (from ticker)
> Here it is! United Zinc up three points on first quote!

> SELBY
> (jubilant)
> We'll own the world!

Paulette emerges from Squeegee's coat, wearing a party hat. She bows a noisemaker which sounds like the noon whistle, heard in the first act. Skinner and Selby, startled, look around. Squeegee, again going on sense memory, plus a large sandwich out of his pocket and starts eating it. Randolph flies in from the window and sits on the table beside Squeegee, creating quite a commotion. Skinner goes to shoe him out. Selby holds him back.

                              SELBY
    Stop, you fool!

                             SKINNER
    Why?

                              SELBY
                              (sotto)
    That may be how he gets his information!

CLOSE SHOT - SQUEEGEE

He pulls a pickle out of another pocket and gives it to Randolph, munching his sandwich.

                                                    DISSOLVE:

FULL SHOT—LOCKER ROOM—NIGHT

Virgil is there alone. He goes to a TV at the end of the locker room, switches it on, picks up a few things on the floor as the set warms up, and then sits down to watch.

CLOSE SHOT—TV SCREEN

A typical TV news commentator appears on the screen...unctuous and voice filled with portents of doom.

                           COMMENTATOR
        And the news this evening remains the
        same...window washer wipes out Wall
        Street.

LONG VIEW—STOCK EXCHANGE FLOOR (STOCK)

There is the usual type of frantic trading going on.

                       COMMENTATOR'S VOICE
        A form of panic continued to grip trading
        on the stock exchange today as the raids
        of the new Wolf of Wall Street intensified.

FULL SHOT—SELBY AND SKINNER OFFICE

All is organized confusion, with the floor deep in ticket tape, men rushing back and forth, and Selby and Skinner barking orders into phones.

>COMMENTATOR'S VOICE
>Here in the investment firm of Selby and Skinner, center of operations for the mysterious ex-window washer, the infallible predictions of one man are spreading fear and confusion throughout the financial world.

CLOSE SHOT—SQUEEGEE

He is smiling his odd smile.

>COMMENTATOR'S VOICE
>Repercussions shake foreign capitals, too.

AIR VIEW—ROME (STOCK)

>COMMENTATOR'S VIEW
>Rome. Demonstrators battle police in bitter street fighting.

FULL VIEW—CROWDS (STOCK)

There is a typical small skirmish between rioters and Italian police/

>COMMENTATOR'S VOICE
>Paris.

FULL VIEW—CROWDS (STOCK)

Crowds demonstrate outside the French Chamber of Deputies.

>COMMENTATOR'S VOICE
>Crowds gather as another French cabinet falls.

AIR VIEW — LONDON (STOCK)

> COMMENTATOR'S VOICE
> And in London, angry questions are asked in the House of Commons.

CLOSE SHOT — MEMBER OF PARLIAMENT

> MP
> (with British reserve)
> I say... who is this Squeegee person?

DISSOLVE:

FULL SHOT — SKINNER AND SELBY OFFICE — DAY

Squeegee, dressed in a cutaway that comes remarkably close to fitting, is sitting in a chair as Skinner pleads with him. Selby is furious with Skinner.

> SKINNER
> (to Squeegee)
> Be reasonable, won't you? I may have made a mistake, but you can pull us out.

> SELBY
> Made a mistake? We were making millions, and *you* had to start playing your own tips!

> SKINNER
> I thought...

> SELBY
> You did?! The world at our feet, and he starts to think!

The secretary appears at the door.

SECRETARY
They're calling for more margin on your Peru Platinum.

SELBY
Stall!

She goes out.

SELBY
You idiot, why did you put a fortune into Peru Platinum?

SKINNER
We can still clean up —
(looks at clock)
fifteen minutes until the market closes.

Selby turns to Squeegee.

SELBY
Please... tell us! Up, or down? Tell us!

SQUEEGEE
No.

SKINNER
Why not?

SQUEEGEE
A week age you promised me fifteen hundred dollars.

SELBY
Fifteen hundred? You're worth millions on paper... millions!

                    SQUEEGEE
               I need fifteen hundred.

                     SKINNER
               I'll write you a check.

                    SQUEEGEE
               Cash.

                      SELBY
               All right, all right! Here!

He takes some large bills out of his wallet and thrusts them at Squeegee.

                     SKINNER
               Now tell us!

                    SQUEEGEE
               Just a minute.

He presses the buzzer on the table. The secretary comes in.

                    SECRETARY
               You wanted me?

Squeegee rises, and walks to her with a slight swagger.

                    SQUEEGEE
               Have them send up a mink coat.

He hands her the money carelessly. She stares at him for a moment, then kisses him on the check and runs out. Squeegee puts his hand to his check, stunned. The other hand strays down near the jealous Paulette. Squeegee yelps suddenly in pain and jerks out his thumb.

                     SKINNER
               The clock, the clock! Peru Platinum! Up,
               or down?

Squeegee returns to the task at hand with the case and assurance of a great general making a tactical decision.

> SQUEEGEE
> Peru Platinum.

> SELBY
> Hurry!

Squeegee suddenly stops, and a look of great surprise comes over his face.

> SKINNER
> What's the matter?

> SQUEEGEE
> Want to hear something funny? I don't know the answer.

> SELBY
> That's the silliest thing I ever heard of!

> SKINNER
> Of course it is! Their board meets today... all you have to do is tell us what the board decides!

> SQUEEGEE
> What's the date?

> SELBY
> The 28th. Why?

Squeegee is trying to piece things together.

> SQUEEGEE
> I always washed Peru Platinum on the 28th. The board meeting.

Selby turns to Squeegee.

SELBY
Please... tell us! Up, or down? Tell us!

SQUEEGEE
No.

SKINNER
Why not?

SQUEEGEE
A week ago you promised me fifteen hundred dollars.

SELBY
Fifteen hundred? You're worth millions on paper... millions!

SQUEEGEE
I need fifteen hundred.

SKINNER
I'll write you a check.

SQUEEGEE
Cash.

SELBY
All right, all right! Here!

He takes some large bills out of his wallet and thrusts them at Squeegee.

SKINNER
Now tell us!

SQUEEGEE
Just a minute.

He presses the buzzer on the table. The secretary comes in.

SECRETARY
You wanted me?

Squeegee rises, and walks to her with a slight swagger.

SQUEEGEE
Have them send up a mink coat.

He hands her the money carelessly. She stares at him for a moment, then kisses him on the check and runs out. Squeegee puts his hand to his check, stunned. The other hand strays down near the jealous Paulette. Squeegee yelps suddenly in pain and jerks out his thumb.

SKINNER
The clock, the clock! Peru Platinum! Up, or down?

Squeegee returns to the task at hand with the case and assurance of a great general making a tactical decision.

SQUEEGEE
Peru Platinum.

SELBY
Hurry!

Squeegee suddenly stops, and a look of great surprise comes over his face.

SKINNER
What's the matter?

SQUEEGEE
Want to hear something funny? I don't know the answer.

SELBY
That's the silliest thing I ever heard of!

SKINNER
Of course it is! Their board meets today…
all you have to do is tell us what the board
decides!

SQUEEGEE
What's the date?

SELBY
The 28th. Why?

Squeegee is trying to piece things together.

SQUEEGEE
I always washed Peru Platinum on the
28th. The board meeting.

SELBY
(it hits him)
They let him listen!

SKINNER
You get information by washing windows?

SQUEEGEE
Well, I couldn't help hearing —

SELBY
But you haven't been on the windows for a week!

SQUEEGEE
I just ran out.

SKINNER
We're ruined!

SELBY
We've got eight minutes! Get out there
and find out!

He rushes Squeegee to the window. Squeegee, about to step out, steps back.

>   SQUEEGEE
>   I can't.
>
>   SKINNER
>   (beside himself)
>   Why not?
>
>   SQUEEGEE
>   Now that I have money, I'm afraid.
>
>   SELBY
>   You haven't got a cent! We're all wiped
>   out! This is our last chance!
>
>   SQUEEGEE
>   Oh.

He steps out.

>   SKINNER
>   Hurry!

FULL SHOT—EXT. BUILDING

CAMERA DOLLIES with Squeegee as he picks his way down the ledge. He stops at the Peru Platinum window, lowers the window and steps half inside.

FULL SHOT—PERU PLATINUM OFFICE

The same board of directors is seated around the table, headed by the mustached financier. All look up when the figure in the cutaway steps in the window. Squeegee finds them all looking at him. Attempting to be casual, he takes out his pocket handkerchief and starts polishing the window.

>   FINANCIER
>   (pointing)
>   El Lobo!

The board members put their heads together, resuming their meeting in low, indistinguishable Spanish. Squeegee loans in, cupping his ear in order to hear.

CLOSE SHOT—SQUEEGEE

As he is leaning in, Paulette's tail comes up under his nose. He endeavors to brush it away with one hand, but with no success.

FULL SHOT—ROOM

The financier stares at Squeegee, in rage.

>FINANCIER
>No man makes the fool of Don Jose... not over El Lobo!

He strides over to the window to close it.

TWO SHOT—FINANCIER AND SQUEEGEE

The financier gets the peanut shell treatment from Paulette. He recoils in bewilderment.

FULL SHOT—SELBY AND SKINNER OFFICE

The two are leaning out the window, trying to see what is happening.

>SKINNER
>Why doesn't he come back?

>SELBY
>Another two minutes and the exchange closes! There's only one thing to do!

>SKINNER
>What's that?

>SELBY
>Go after him!

SKINNER
Are you mad? 76 floors up?

SELBY
Would you rather be wiped out?

SKINNER
I'll follow you.

Selby steps out, followed by Skinner, who clings to him.

FULL SHOT—EXT. BUILDING

The two climb out on the ledge, clinging to each other.

SELBY
Don't look down!

SKINNER
I won't.

He takes a look.

LONG VIEW—STREET BELOW (STOCK)

MED. SHOT—LEDGE

Skinner sways, and grabs Selby.

SELBY
What happened?

SKINNER
I looked!

They inch their way along the ledge, their feet slipping several times.

SKINNER
Are we almost there?

                        SELBY
            There's the window!

                        SKINNER
            Where's Squeegee?

                        SELBY
            Gone!

They look at each other.

                        SKINNER
            What do we do now?

                        SELBY
            Go back.

Skinner looks along the narrow ledge they have traversed, then looks down.

LONG VIEW—STREET BELOW (STOCK)

MED. SHOT—LEDGE

Skinner covers his eyes with his hands and grabs Selby.

                        SKINNER
            I can't go back!

FULL SHOT—LEDGE

Squeegee sticks his head out of the Skinner and Selby window.

                        SQUEEGEE
            I couldn't find out anything! But it didn't
            matter... the market's closed!

TWO SHOT—SKINNER AND SELBY

They are clinging together.

                    SKINNER
Cleaned out.

                    SELBY
Stripped to the bone. And I gave that idiot
fifteen hundred of my own money.

                    SKINNER
As long as we're broke, what are we
waiting for?

They both look down, but neither one has the courage. They try to inch along the ledge, but stop. Squeegee then appears on the ledge beside them.

                    SQUEEGEE
Come on, gentlemen... you'll catch cold
out here.

                    SKINNER
I can't walk back!

He shivers. Squeegee backs up to him.

                    SQUEEGEE
Hold onto my belt... I'll load you back.

CLOSE SHOT—PAULETTE

She is undoing Squeegee's belt buckle.

FULL SHOT—LEDGE

                    SQUEEGEE
               (over his shoulder)
     All set?

He walks jauntily along the ledge and in the window. Selby, horror-stricken, is left holding his belt. Skinner is holding onto Selby. They both begin to sway. At the last minute Squeegee reaches out with his umbrella and hooks Selby's neck, and hauls them both to the window and safety.

> SKINNER
> (emotionally)
> You saved us! Why!

> SQUEEGEE
> It's my only belt.

He takes it delicately from Selby.

FADE OUT

TAG FOR SPONSOR

FADE IN:

MED. SHOT—LOCKER ROOM—DAY

Virgil is seated on a desk in the locker room.

> VIRGIL
> Well, after that we had to take Squeegee off Wall Street for a while. Not that he got along better anywhere else. There was the day he washed windows at that girls' school. And when we sent him to wax the floor at Roseland. Not to mention the day he cleaned up at the U.N. But whatever he does, everybody loves him.

Squeegee moves across in front of Virgil, looking back, and then breaking into a run. Following him, with murder in their eyes, are the entire case of the elevator scene. Virgil looks after them, and then faces front.

> VIRGIL
> See what I mean?

FADE OUT

FADE IN:

FULL SHOT—RECEPTION ROOM—DAY

Squeegee comes in through the door, in his old window washer's outfit, carrying his squeegee and bucket. The Secretary rises and comes toward him with open arms, wearing the mink coat. Squeegee starts to hold out his arms.

OFFICE—ANOTHER ANGLE

The secretary sweeps right past him into the arms of the handsome man of the night club scene.

CLOSE SHOT—SQUEEGEE

He looks at them: Paulette emerges. Squeegee strokes her head, then goes on through the other door.

FADE OUT

THE END

TAG FOR SPONSOR

FADE IN:

134 MED. SHOT—LOCKER ROOM—DAY

BearManor Media
PO Box 71426 • Albany, GA 31708

FOR ALL THESE BOOKS AND MORE VISIT
BEARMANORMEDIA.COM

Coming in September!

HOLD THAT JOAN
BY BEN OHMART
Finally, a biography of one of the funniest, most overlooked comediennes of the 20th century. The star of television's *I Married Joan* and the film classics *Hold That Ghost*, *Show Business*, *Thin Ice* and many more, very little has been documented about Joan's comical career — until now.
ISBN 1-59393-046-1
$24.95 + $3 US P&H

TALKING TO THE PIANO PLAYER
BY STUART ODERMAN
Interviews with Marlene Dietrich, Frank Capra, Colleen Moore, Jackie Coogan, Madge Bellamy, Aileen Pringle, Allan Dwan, Adela Rogers St. Johns, Douglas Fairbanks, Jr., and more!
ISBN: 1-59393-013-5
$19.95 + $3 US P&H

THE FIRESIGN THEATRE
BY FREDERICK C. WIEBEL, JR.
The only book you'll ever need about the past/present/future masters of American satire. The utterly futile yet complete history of The Firesign Theatre and its also complete recording history is bundled together in one too-large book!
ISBN: 1-59393-043-7. $29.95 + $3 US P&H

NAMES YOU NEVER REMEMBER, WITH FACES YOU NEVER FORGET
BY JUSTIN HUMPHREYS
Illustrated with over 100 photographs, Names interviews the unsung character men who often outshone the stars that surrounded them.
ISBN 1-59393-041-0
$19.95 + $3 US P&H

Presenting the best in nostalgia and entertainment books...
www.BearManorMedia.com
1-800-566-1251 (Order line only)

BearManor Media
PO Box 71426 • Albany, GA 31708

FOR ALL THESE BOOKS AND MORE VISIT
BEARMANORMEDIA.COM

LINGERIE FOR HOOKERS IN THE SNOW
BY WALT DISNEY SINGER ROBIE LESTER
An Audiography by Robie Lester. For 7 years she was the Disneyland Records story reader. And don't forget the singing voice for Eva Gabor in *The Aristocats*. Now you can read along and listen to this famous voice actress' musical cues in her OWN book/CD!
ISBN: 1-59393-058-5
$16.95 + $2.50 US P&H

WE BOMBED IN NEW LONDON
THE INSIDE STORY OF THE BROADWAY MUSICAL LATE NITE COMIC by Brian Gari
Eddie Cantor's grandson's true story of one man's tenacious plight to get his musical mounted. From its romantic inception to its eventual demise and the score's resurrection in cabarets and recordings, this book takes you on a journey through the ups and downs of the theatrical world with all its excitement, disappointment, laughter and hope.
ISBN: 1-59393-051-8
$19.95 + $2.50 US P&H

VIC & SADE
BY BILL IDELSON
Long-time cast member Bill Idelson has penned the first history of the beloved radio show, *Vic & Sade*. Complete with a prolific amount of script excerpts and photos from his personal collection, this is the perfect book for all you Vic and Sadists out there!
ISBN: 1-59393-061-5
$24.95+ $3 US P&H

NOT SO DUMB
THE LIFE AND CAREER OF MARIE WILSON
BY CHARLES TRANBERG
Ready for the first biography on blonde, bubbly Marie Wilson? Was she really that vapid? Well—read the book on this *My Friend Irma* star for just $19.95 + $2.50 US postage and find out!
ISBN: 1-59393-049-6

Presenting the best in nostalgia and entertainment books...
www.BearManorMedia.com
1-800-566-1251 (Order line only)

www.ingramcontent.com/pod-product-compliance
Lightning Source LLC
Chambersburg PA
CBHW022104160426
43198CB00008B/348